SO YOU WANT TO DO CRAFT SHOWS...

16 Lessons I Learned Doing Craft Shows

by Warren Feld

SO YOU WANT TO DO CRAFT SHOWS...
16 Lessons I Learned Doing Craft Shows

by Warren Feld

Learn How To...

...Find, Evaluate and Select Craft Shows Right for You
...Determine a Set of Realistic Goals
...Compute a Simple Break-Even Analysis
...Develop Your Applications and Apply
in the Smartest Ways
...Understand How Much Inventory to Bring
... Set Up and Present Both Yourself and Your Wares
... Best Promote and Operate Your Craft Show Business

Warren Feld Jewelry, Publisher
www.warrenfeldjewelry.com
2022

SO YOU WANT TO DO CRAFT SHOWS
by Warren Feld

Copyright Page

Published by
Warren Feld Jewelry
718 Thompson Ln, Ste 123
Nashville, TN 37204
www.warrenfeldjewelry.com

Cover by Warren Feld. Showing *Susan Thorton, Thorton Metal Studios (https://www.thorntonmetals.com), doing one of the things she does best.*

ISBN: 979-8-9865354-0-1 E-book
ISBN: 979-8-9865354-1-8 Kindle E-Book
ISBN: 979-8-9865354-2-5 Print

Library of Congress Control Number: 2022912538

TABLE OF CONTENTS

What You Will Learn

In this book, I discuss critical choices jewelry designers need to make when doing craft shows.

It is very important for anyone thinking about selling at craft shows, festivals, bazaars, markets, or similar settings to be smart about it.

That means, understanding everything involved, and asking the right questions.

Learn How To...

...Find, Evaluate and Select Craft Shows Right For You
...Set Realistic Goals
...Compute a Simple Break-Even Analysis
...Best Develop Your Applications and Apply
...Understand How Much Inventory To Bring
... Set Up and Present Both Yourself and Your Wares

Doing craft shows is a wonderful experience. You can make a lot of money. You meet new people. You have new adventures. And you learn a lot about business and arts and crafts designing.

I know you are eager to begin. Let's get started.

NOTE: This book is also available as a video tutorial. *Click here* (https://so-you-want-to-be-a-jewelry-designer.teachable.com/p/so-you-want-to-do-craft-shows)**.** https://so-you-want-to-be-a-jewelry-designer.teachable.com/p/so-you-want-to-do-craft-shows

Intro To Book
and Acknowledgements

For Jayden Alfre Jones
Jewelry Designer
Life Partner

Also, you might be interested in my SO YOU WANT TO DO CRAFT SHOWS video tutorial (https://so-you-want-to-be-a-jewelry-designer.teachable.com/p/so-you-want-to-do-craft-shows) *online.*
https://so-you-want-to-be-a-jewelry-designer.teachable.com/p/so-you-want-to-do-craft-shows

In the late 1980s, Jayden and I began our jewelry making adventure. First, a garage sale to test out our ideas. We combined Jayden's artisan jewelry with jewelry making parts and laid them out on the lawn in front of our apartment. Incredibly successful. $6000.00! I worried, what if this was a fluke? So six weeks later, we did it again. We duplicated the finished jewelry and the selection of jewelry making parts, and held another garage sale. Again, a success at $4700.00.

So we took the plunge and rented a booth at the Nashville Flea Market, one of the granddaddy flea markets of all flea markets across the nation. New vendors begin in outside stalls. Every month we hauled our merchandise, our tables, our displays, our chairs, our food and water, and our heater or fan, depending on the time of year. Grueling. Very grueling. But profitable.

Between the monthly shows, we busily made more and more jewelry. We ordered more and more parts to sell.

And loaded the van. Drove to the fairgrounds. Unloaded. Set up. Shivered or sweated. And hawked our goods.

About a year later, an indoor flea market opened up nearby. You had a booth that you could close up and lock up. The market was open Wednesday through Sunday every week, and you had to be there or forfeit your booth. This took some pressure off in that we didn't have to pack up and load up and unload and unpack. This also allowed us to make and repair jewelry onsite.

Another year later, we were in a storefront in downtown Nashville. Several weekends each year we did one or another art and craft show or bead show.

The rest is history. But you never forget your roots.

Craft Shows Are Great Opportunities

There are many advantages to doing craft shows.

- You can make good money.
- You can jump-start and enhance your reputation

- You can learn a lot of good business tricks
- And find out about a lot of good resources

If,... And that's a big, "If!" You know what you're doing.

All too often, jewelry designers who want to do craft shows have not done their homework. They have not researched and evaluated which shows to do, and which not to do. They have not figured out how best to set up their booths and displays. They are clueless about what inventory to make, and to bring, and how to price it. They are unprepared to promote, to market and to sell.

I developed this book to help prepare you for doing this kind of craft show homework.

I discuss:
- What information you need to gather
- How to set personal and business goals
- How to find, evaluate and select craft shows
- And, how best to promote and operate your business at these craft shows.

In fact, I go over 16 lessons I learned for successfully doing craft shows.

I have divided these into two groups.

First, I discuss lessons about finding and selecting craft shows. These lessons are about How to find craft shows, and determine how well you and your business will fit in.

The second group of lessons are about how to promote and operate your business at these craft shows. These lessons focus on booth set-up, how best to organize all the various tasks involved, how to promote your business, how to manage money, and how to make sales.

Then I offer some final words of advice.

At the end of the book, I have a page of internet resources links for you to explore in more detail.

Thank You

In 2000, we organized a community group made up of jewelry making instructors, advanced students, and bead store staff. They were tasked with coming up with a design-focused educational curriculum useful for bead stringing, bead weaving and wire working. The goal was to come up with something that takes the student beyond craft – that is, beyond merely following a set of step-by-step instructions. It was important to educate students on both aesthetic, artistic requirements as well as architectural, functional ones. This group did an excellent job.

I want to thank the community group for their hard and insightful work, but particularly Connie Welch, who spearheaded many ideas and efforts.

There was great interest in business-oriented classes for our beading and jewelry making students. Many of them did craft shows, bazaars, flea markets and the like. This book emerged from both my experiences doing these shows, as well as working with these students as they established their own businesses.

Special thanks to the original masterminds behind the Intergalactic Bead Shows. They provided lots of insights and advice for doing craft shows, as well as lots of stories of things gone awry. You learn a lot from mistakes and responses to unexpected situations.

Another special thanks to Susan Thorton. Her business Thorton Metal Studios (https://www.thorntonmetals.com) prominently featured in many local art and craft shows in Nashville. She always impressed me that she knew the best ways to find shows, develop saleable inventories, display her wares, set up her booth, and entice customers to buy her pieces. I have always held her up as the best example for doing things the right way.

Other Books By Warren Feld

So You Want To Be A Jewelry Designer

Becoming a Jewelry Designer is exciting. With each

piece, you are challenged with this profound question: *Why does some jewelry draw people's attention, and others do not?* Yes there are some craft and art aspects to jewelry making. But when jewelry designers turn to how-to books or art theory texts, however, these do not uncover the necessary answers. They do not show you how to make trade-offs between beauty and function. Nor how to introduce your pieces publicly. You get insufficient practical guidance about knowing when your piece is finished and successful. In short, you do not learn about *design.* You do not learn the essentials about how to go beyond basic mechanics, anticipate the wearer's understandings and desires, or gain management control over the process. *So You Want To Be A Jewelry Designer* reinterprets how to apply techniques and modify art theories from the Jewelry Designer's perspective. This very detailed book reveals how to become literate and fluent in jewelry design.

The major topics covered include,

1. Jewelry Beyond Craft: Gaining A Disciplinary Literacy and Fluency in Design

2. Getting Started

3. What Is Jewelry, Really?

4. Materials, Techniques and Technologies

5. Rules of Composition, Construction and Manipulation

6. Design Management

7. Introducing Your Designs Publicly

8. Developing Those Intuitive Skills Within: Creativity, Inspiration and Aspiration, Passion

9. Jewelry In Context

10 Teaching Disciplinary Literacy In Jewelry Design

Order: https://www.amazon.com/So-You-Want-Jewelry-Designer/dp/B09Y3VNNMW/ref=tmm_pap_swatch_0?encoding=UTF8&qid=1653169170&sr=8-1

Conquering The Creative Marketplace

Many people learn beadwork and jewelry-making in order to sell the pieces they make. Based both on the creation and development of my own jewelry design business, as well as teaching countless students over the past 35+ years about business and craft, I want to address what should be some of your key concerns and uncertainties. I want to share with you the kinds of things (specifically, *a business mindset* and confidence) it takes to start your own jewelry business, run it, anticipate risks and rewards, and lead it to a level of success you feel is right for you. I want to help you plan your road map.

I will explore answers to such questions as: How does someone get started marketing and selling their pieces?

What business fundamentals need to be brought to the fore? How do you measure risk and return on investment? How does the creative person develop and maintain a passion for business? To what extent should business decisions affect artistic choices? What similar traits to successful jewelry designers do those in business share? How do you protect your intellectual property?

The major topics covered include,

1. Integrating Business With Design

2. Getting Started

3. Financial Management

4. Product Development, Creating Your Line, and Pricing

5. Marketing, Promotion, Branding

6. Selling

7. Professional Responsibilities and Strategic Planning

8. Professional Responsibilities and Gallery / Boutique Representation

9. Professional Responsibilities and Creating Your Necessary Written Documents

Thank you. I hope you found this introduction useful.

Also, check out my website (www.warrenfeldjewelry.com).

Enroll in my jewelry design and business of craft Video Tutorials (https://so-you-want-to-be-a-jewelry-designer.teachable.com/p/home) online.

Begin with my ORIENTATION TO BEADS & JEWELRY FINDINGS COURSE https://so-you-want-to-be-a-jewelry-designer.teachable.com/

Follow my articles on Medium.com. https://medium.com/@warren-29626

Subscribe to my Learn To Bead blog (https://blog.landofodds.com).

Visit Land of Odds online for all your jewelry making supplies. (https://www.landofodds.com)

Check out my Jewelry Making and Beadwork Kits
(https://www.landofodds.com/kits/)

Artist Statement
(http://www.warrenfeldjewelry.com/wfjartiststatement.ht
ml)

Teaching Statement
(http://www.warrenfeldjewelry.com/pdf/TEACHING%20S
TATEMENT.pdf)

Portfolio
(http://www.warrenfeldjewelry.com/pdf/PORTFOLIO.pdf
)

Testimonials
(http://www.warrenfeldjewelry.com/pdf/TESTIMONIALS.
pdf)

Video Tutorials
(https://so-you-want-to-be-a-jewelry-
designer.teachable.com/)

Design Philosophy
(http://www.warrenfeldjewelry.com/wfjdesignapproach.ht
m)

Add your name to my *email list*
https://mailchi.mp/4032bd33748d/so-you-want-to-be-a-jewelry-designer

---

LESSON 1:
Not Every Craft Show Is Alike

Meet Roland and Rolanda. New to the jewelry designing trade. When they started, they decided to apply to every local craft show and festival and flea market they could find. They set up at the St. Bernard's Festival. The Metro Arts Commission "In The Park" Program. The South 2nd Street Flea Market. And the Flea Market at Houser Lake. And the Tennessee Arts Commission Fair. And the Craft Show of the Americas.

Roland and Rolanda did not understand that every

craft show was not alike. They were not prepared for the conflicting demands, and their business suffered for it.

Craft shows and similar venues are places where you can bring your merchandise, set up some kind of display, and sell to people walking by.

Craft shows are a great way to make money. People come to craft shows to buy. Craft shows are a great way to get broad exposure to a large customer base. They are a great way to jump-start, re-start and re-energize your jewelry design (or other art or craft) business. And, sometimes you will meet people there who own businesses where they want to buy your items for re-sale.

Craft shows allow you to have little investment in overhead, like rent, insurance and the like that comes with a physical store. Craft shows mean you do not have to share your profits with a store or gallery.

But, for Roland and Rolanda, and for lots of people, it's important to understand that not every craft show is alike.

There are many types of shows, including,

- Art and crafts shows

- Flea markets and bazaars

- Festivals and fairs

- Juried vs. open

- Indoor vs. outdoor

- Holiday or themed

- Large vs. small operations

- Walk-by-booth setups vs. walk-in-booth setups

- Mixed merchandise vs. jewelry only shows

It is important to become familiar with each of these. Let's examine them in more detail...

ARTS AND CRAFTS SHOWS

One type is an *Arts and Crafts Show*. These are professionally-produced shows which promote the sales of handcrafted art and other craft items. These can be inside or outside. You find them in a wide assortment of settings, from parks to community centers to shopping malls. Some focus on art to the exclusion of craft. Others have a broader focus.

This type of show works well for jewelry artists. Arts and Crafts Shows attract a lot of people who expect to pay for quality and who come to buy.

But be careful that these shows are not "top-heavy" with jewelry vendors, unless, of course, it is a jewelry-only show.

The application process is often formal, and sometimes juried. Some entry fees are very low. Others very high.

FLEA MARKETS AND BAZAARS

Flea Markets and Bazaars are typically organized by churches, schools, clubs or organizations. Often with a fund-raising purpose in mind.

There are also businesses in many communities that, for a small fee, offer a place for anyone to come and sell their wares.

There are very few rules for entry, and fees tend to be very low.

The mix of what is for sale can be very haphazard.

People often come looking for bargains, or to browse.

In many cases, the attendance will have highs and lows during each day.

This type of show works well for the crafter or hobbyist who makes things during the year, and wants a once-a-year sales outlet.

Usually, I find that the return-on-investment (ROI) for these kinds of shows is not very good. However, it depends on history, timing, weather and location. For example, a bazaar sets up every two months at a local university where I live. They charge $25.00 for a weekend booth rental. And people doing this bazaar usually make a killing.

FESTIVALS AND FAIRS

Festivals and Fairs are "Special Events", sponsored by towns, civic groups, or neighborhood associations, and often put on by a special promoter. These are well-organized, well-publicized and attract lots of people.

Sometimes these will take the form of an arts and crafts show, and that will be their central purpose. Othertimes, the main purpose is some kind of entertainment, and they have an area set aside for people to sell their wares.

If the promoters emphasize the arts and crafts part of the festival, then you can do well here. People at festivals are typically willing to spend at mid-range prices.

If there is little promotion of arts and crafts, or, if that area set aside for arts and crafts sales is far from the main action, then this may not work out well for you.

JURIED OR OPEN ADMISSION

Some shows are *open to all takers* who pay the entry fee. Other shows are *juried*. That is, they require that you submit images of your work, and perhaps, some kind of artist statement. A panel of judges reviews your work, and decides whom to admit to the show.

Juried shows may also require that you submit images of your booth and display set up.

Juried shows have good control over the quality of vendors, as well as the mix of merchandise available for sale. The fees can be steep. If these juried shows have a good reputation and history, they can be very lucrative. They are big reputation builders for you, as well.

INDOOR OR OUTDOOR

Some shows are held *indoors*. Here you have some protection from the weather. Other shows are held *outdoors*, where you do not.

On good weather days, people like to be outdoors. On bad weather days, people like to be indoors.

What you bring and how you set up will vary a bit between indoor and outdoor. You can often spread out a little more, when outdoors.

You will have different special lighting needs indoors than outdoors.

If the indoor show is very well attended, it can get very claustrophobic, dusty and hot.

If the weather gets really bad or unpredictable, you might have a poor showing at an outdoor show.

Be sure to ask the show promoters what their policy is for inclement weather, if the show is outdoors.

HOLIDAY, THEMED OR
TIMING SENSITIVE SHOWS

Some shows have a strong *theme* which sets a very important tone and direction for the show. You need to pay close attention to this theme.

There are Christmas shows and Western shows and Native American shows. There are Summer Celebrations and Winter Celebrations. There are Ethnic Festivals. Town History Festivals. Historical re-enactments. Lots of shows and festivals and bazaars with a holiday or other theme, or something tied to a specific time or event.

Make sure the merchandise you bring, and how you set up your displays and signage, and even the way you present yourself as an artist and craftsperson, coordinates well with the theme.

LARGE VS. SMALL OPERATION

Some operations are *large*, and others are *small*.

Obviously, the larger they are, the more people they will attract, and the more likely they will sustain themselves over time. That means less risk for you.

However, if the operation is small… such as, a small number of vendors, or a limited range or quantity of merchandise, or a smaller expected attendance, or, minimal advertising and promotion, then it poses more risk, from a business sense. So, when setting up at a small operation, be sure there are some other compensating factors, such as a special location, or that it is linked to a very special event, or that the attendees are primed to spend, and spend a lot.

WALK-BY OR WALK-IN BOOTHS

Some shows let you set up some kind of booth, where customers can walk into. We call this a *walk-in setup*. Other shows line up rows of tables. You rent one or more tables. The tables, from vendor to vendor, usually merge with one another. Customers work their way past the front of these rows of tables. We call this a *walk-by setup*.

I prefer walk-in setups. These give you much better control and management of customers and the buying situation. They more clearly delineate the boundaries of your booth, from those of your neighbors.

If doing a walk-by setup, then, if you can secure a

corner space, or a central aisle intersection, or a spot near the main entrance, these work better. They give you more visibility. It's all about visibility.

If you can afford to rent more than one table, and have the inventory to display on more than 1 table, this gives you even more visibility. The more visibility you have, the better your sales.

JEWELRY ONLY VS. MIX OF MERCHANDISE

Most shows showcase a *mix of merchandise*. However, some shows are *jewelry only*.

When it is jewelry only, the show attracts buyers specifically interested in jewelry, but this will be a smaller number of buyers who might attend a mixed-merchandise show. If you are selling at a jewelry only show, be sure something about your work sets you apart from the crowd.

When it is a mix of merchandise show, it may be a little more difficult to link up to your target customer. However, there will be more potential customers overall.

Shows which have a mix of merchandise often have to limit the number of jewelry vendors -- jewelry is an especially popular category.

BROAD OR NARROW OR LIMITED ADVERTISING AND PROMOTION

At the show, you are dependent on attendance. That means, you are dependent on how well the show promoters deliver the goods.

How much money do they spend on advertising and marketing...

... to get the word out?

How much effort are they making...
... to earn a good reputation?

Indigenous art features at fair

By MATT MALONEY

THE Tasmanian Craft Fair will premiere an Aboriginal art exhibition at historic Deloraine manor Peppers Calstock.

Curated by Northern Territory gallery Central Art, the collection will comprise work from more than 20 Central and Western Desert Aboriginal artists, including Minnie Pwerle, Emily Pwerle, Walangkura Napanangka and George Tjungurrayi.

Central Art director Sabine Haider said pieces in the Tradition to Modernity exhibition had been selected to resonate with the historic property and the Meander Valley surrounds.

Fair director John Dare said the event had secured the 3 Nations: Asian Contemporary Glass Art exhibition, which will visit Australia for the first time in October and feature unique Chinese, Japanese and Korean glasswork.

Mr Dare said there were 70 new stalls and exhibitions among the 250 that would be spread over 14 Deloraine locations.

Among these is the Gourmet Festival, which will showcase Tasmanian produce.

In its 30th year, the fair will see stallholders and exhibitors spread across 14 different venues at Deloraine.

Last year, 36,000 people were estimated to have passed through the town during the event. Since the not-for-profit event started, more than $2 million has been raised for Deloraine community projects.

So, shows with large marketing budgets do better than those with small ones. Established shows do much, much better than 1st year shows. In fact, I would avoid doing shows in their 1st or 2nd years, until I saw that they were succeeding on some level.

Craft Show Marketing Budget	Q1	Q2	Q3	Q4	TOTALS
Public Relations					
PR Firm					$
Press Release Development					$
Press release wire fees					$
Press Kit Materials					$
Review Program					$
Analyst subscriptions/reports					$
Press tour(s)					$
TOTAL Public Relations	$	$	$	$	$
Web Marketing					
Online advertising creative					$
Google AdWords program					$
Yahoo ad program					$
Microsoft ad program					$
Search Engine Optimization (SEO)					$
Website development/updates					$
TOTAL Web Marketing	$	$	$	$	$
Advertising					
Creative development					$
Print advertising placements					$
VAR/Channel advertising					$
Radio advertising					$
Television advertising					$
TOTAL Advertising	$	$	$	$	$

I would also closely examine the show's marketing budget. It may be large, but they may be planning to spend all their money on a single billboard along the interstate highway. This is not enough. You want to see the show promoters undertaking a multimethod marketing plan.

WHOLESALE TRADE VS. RETAIL TRADE

Finally, while most shows would be considered *retail* shows, that is, targeted at the general public, some shows are for the *wholesale* trade. That is, businesses who shop wholesale shows are looking for lines of merchandise to carry. These businesses have their own retail outlets for re-selling your work.

28

The fees for these shows are usually very steep. You also need to be prepared operationally to accept and deliver on large orders in a timely manner.

Often, two or more businesses will share the costs of a single booth.

Also, you might be interested in my SO YOU WANT TO DO CRAFT SHOWS video tutorial https://so-you-want-to-be-a-jewelry-designer.teachable.com/p/so-you-want-to-do-craft-shows

LESSON 2:
Research All Your Possibilities

"I heard it through the grapevine". That should be Imogene McAllister Rosenstein's song. Because that's how she finds her craft shows.

By word of mouth.
By Tweet
By Facebook Post
From friends and friends of friends and family of friends of friends.

Like I say, she heard it through the grapevine.

She kept saying to me, "I heard such and such a show was great," or "Have you heard anything about it?" Rarely ever.

She would sign up for things in parts of town that none of her customers would go to.

She was literally all over the place.

There are plenty of tools and resources for finding out which craft shows are right for you. You just have to make yourself aware of these... And use them.

See the last section in this book on HELPFUL RESOURCES.

FINDING THEM: CRAFT SHOW DIRECTORIES

There are many online craft show directories. There are directories of shows in...

- Consumer craft and beading magazines

- Craft and art organizations, associations and clubs, in their newsletters, on their websites and Facebook pages

- Sometimes craft shows will take out ads in local papers looking for vendors

- Local and State arts commissions also might maintain a directory

You can also attend local shows and talk with management. You can talk to various vendors at local shows. You can contact local craft and fine artists.

Online Services

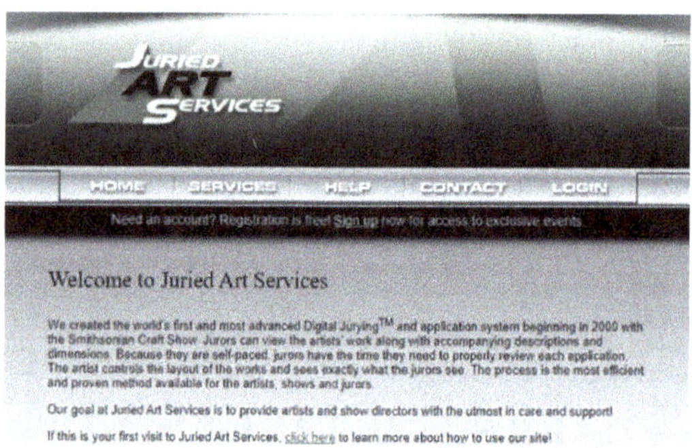

There are also services online which help craft shows find you. For example, *Juried Art Services* (https://www.juriedartservices.com)

(https://www.juriedartservices.com) or *Zapplication (https://www.zapplication.org)*.

These digital juried and application systems allow you to post a profile with images online. They send out email calls for applications from craft shows they represent. And they allow you to tailor fit your application to the requirements of that specific show.

You register with these online, uploading images of your work, images of your booth and display, and various write-ups.

LESSON 3:
Know Which Craft Shows Are For You

Rowena Starlight liked to tell everyone she lived on Light House Road. She might as well have been living in outer Mongolia. She was determined to sell high-end jewelry in low-brow settings. She spent so much time making each piece of jewelry, and so little time researching where to sell it. She rarely sold anything. Sad for her, she couldn't figure out why.

NOT EVERY CRAFT SHOW WILL BE FOR YOU.

When you research show opportunities, ask yourself:

Is there a good fit with

- Your merchandise

- Your goals

- Your expectations

- Your customers?

Evaluate all your show options before selecting one or more of them.

MAKE SITE VISITS

Scope it out before committing to it.

If you can't attend a show prior to applying, ask the promoter for names and phone numbers or email addresses of a few of the exhibitors that have done the show before, and are returning again.

You want to ask and have answered a series of questions:

Questions to ask yourself
Questions to ask other vendors
Questions to ask the show promoters

ASK YOURSELF THESE QUESTIONS

You are on your site visit.

Carefully observe and ask yourself these questions:

- Is the vendor area the focus of the show, or a part of a larger entertainment venue?

- Is there entertainment?

- Are there food vendors?

- Who is the customer?

- Is there good attendance?

- Is there an admission charge?

- Is there adequate customer parking?

- What is the merchandise mix, and how much is jewelry?

- What is the quality of the merchandise like?

- Is the merchandise hand-crafted only, mostly hand-crafted, or not?

Speak with the vendors, and ask them:

- How well does the show work for them?

- How did they find out about the show?

- Are they satisfied with the management and marketing of the show?

- Are there other vendors, perhaps too many other vendors, selling the same kind of thing?

- What are the best shows they have done, and how does this one compare?

- Would they return to this show and do it again?

SPEAK WITH PROMOTERS

If you can speak with the promoters, ask them:

- How long have they been doing shows, and this show in particular?

- What are their goals for the show?

- What kind of marketing and promotion do they do?

- What is the average attendance?

- What amount does the typical customer spend?

- What are the fees?

- Do you take any additional commissions, such as a percent of sales?

- How are local and state sales taxes (or other taxes) handled?

- Are there any insurance requirements?

- What is involved with the application process?

- Tell them what you sell, and ask them if they think you would fit in?

- If you want to do the next show, when should

you
apply?

- Can you choose your booth location?

- Can you do demonstrations in your booth?

Finally, ask them to add your name to their mailing list!

THINK!

Then, check for show reviews, ratings and experiences on line. Do some social networking.

And, *THINK!*

- How *comfortable* are you with the location

- The *setting*

- The *lay-out*

- The *opportunity*

- The *possibilities* to make a profit

How does your merchandise stack up against that which you have seen?

Try to visualize the event in your mind, with as much information you have gathered.

Is this particular event for you?

Does this show attract the types of customers most likely to buy what you make?

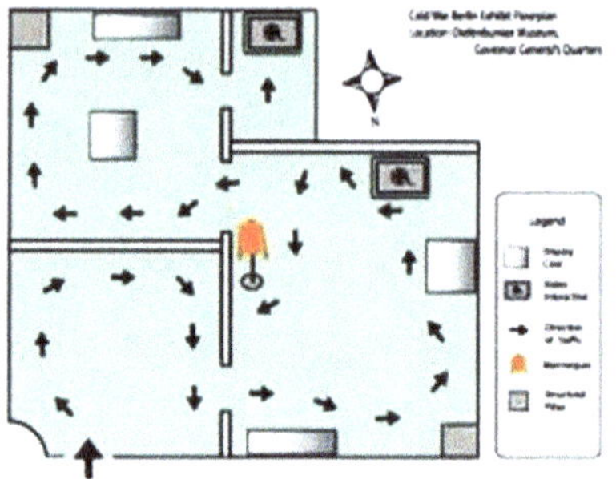

craft show traffic flow

LESSON 4:
Set Realistic Goals /
Determine Break-Even Point

Making money at fairs and shows isn't as easy as it seems. As Roland and Rolanda quickly found out.

They thought all it took was to rent a table at any show or fair, lay out their jewelry, wait for customers to come by, and purchase their stuff.

All through the shows, they sat on chairs reading books, waiting for people to come by. They spent more money on inventory, packing, displays and travel than they ever made.

And they never developed any kind of plan of action.

Roland and Rolanda needed to set realistic goals:

1. How much money did they have to get started and sustain themselves?

2. What was their break-even point?

3. What did they need to prepare themselves to *sell*?

4. What amount of repeat business and follow-up sales were they looking for?

BUDGET

How much money will you need?

Make a list of all possible costs. There are the obvious like transportation, lodging and meals, and the costs of displays, packing and marketing, and the costs of the parts used to make the pieces which sell.

Entry fees will vary widely from show to show. They could cost $25/day up to $400 and up per day. They could go as high as $5000 per day.

Fees		
Auto-Travel		
Food		
Lodging		
Staffing		
Display Supplies		
Marketing Supplies		
Packing Supplies		
Credit Card Fees		
Cell Phone Charges		
Costs of Inventory Sold		

If you have a specific craft show in mind, review their rules, and what they entry fees cover, and do not cover.

What are the costs of extras, like electricity, tables, special lighting? Do they also collect a percent of sales? Do they offer special services, like booth sitting, for extra fees? Is parking free, or do they charge? Do you need to provide additional insurance? Will you need to purchase special licenses, registration and permits, such as an out-of-state wholesale license?

THERE ARE TWO TYPES OF COSTS TO ACCOUNT FOR:

Fixed Costs and ***Variable Costs***

FIXED COSTS:

You have to pay these, whether you make any money or not

ITEM	RATE	CALCULATED COST
FOOD / DRINK	$40.00/day	=$ 80.00
AUTO-TRAVEL	$110.00	=$110.00
LODGING	$65.00	=$ 65.00
FEES	$120.00	=$120.00
STAFFING	$80.00/day	=$160.00
TOTAL FIXED COSTS		=$535.00

VARIABLE COSTS:

You only pay these based on the number of items you sell

ITEM	RATE	CALCULATED COST
SUPPLIES-DISPLAY	5% Inventory Sold (typically 1-5%)	To be calculated
SUPPLIES-MARKETING	12% Inventory Sold (typically 5-15%)	To be calculated
SUPPLIES-PACKING	2% Inventory Sold (typically 1-2%)	To be calculated
CREDIT CARD FEES	5% Inventory Sold (typically 2-5%)	To be calculated
CELL PHONE FEES	1% Inventory Sold (typically 1-2%)	To be calculated
COSTS INVENTORY SOLD	40% Inventory Sold (typically 35-60%)	To be calculated
TOTAL VARIABLE COSTS		To be calculated

You need to prepare a budget to be sure you can pay for what you are committing yourself to.

You will need display supplies, packing supplies, marketing and promotion supplies, and probably some food and drink for yourself. You will be traveling. You may have to stay overnight somewhere. You will probably have some credit card finance charges and cell-phone charges associated with sales you make. You may need to pay someone to help you staff your booth. You probably will be paying various fees – entry, electricity, table rental. And you will need enough money to buy enough supplies to make up your inventory.

**Your breakeven point is when
*your revenues = your costs.***

How much money do you want to make?

At the very least, you want to come home from the show and breakeven. That is, you want to cover all your costs.

So, in your budget, you have begun to list all your costs.

Now, how much inventory will you need to make, and sell, in order to breakeven?

Inventory:
Bring 4x what you need to sell

At this point, we are going to talk about inventory ***in terms of retail prices***, not in terms of numbers of items, and not in terms of wholesale costs.

Our total inventory would equal the total of all retail prices *(=the prices you are selling each piece at)*, if every piece sold.

A good ***rule of thumb*** for figuring out how much inventory to bring is this:

You will need to bring with you, at a minimum, ***4 times the inventory (=total retail dollars) you hope to sell***.

Again,

YOU WILL NEED TO BRING WITH YOU,
AT A MINIMUM,
4 TIMES THE INVENTORY
YOU HOPE TO SELL.

For example, if you need to sell $200.00 of merchandise to breakeven, you will need to bring $800.00 of merchandise with you. Again, $800.00 is the total of all the retail prices of what you bring.

If you want to take in another $100.00 of sales on top of your breakeven, then you will need to sell $300.00 (=$200 + $100) of merchandise, and then you will need to bring a total of $1200.00 (=$800+$400, that is, 4 times $300) of inventory.

This is $400.00 more inventory that you would need to bring to make one hundred more dollars over your breakeven point. Again, $1200.00 is the total of all the retail prices.

BREAKEVEN ANALYSIS

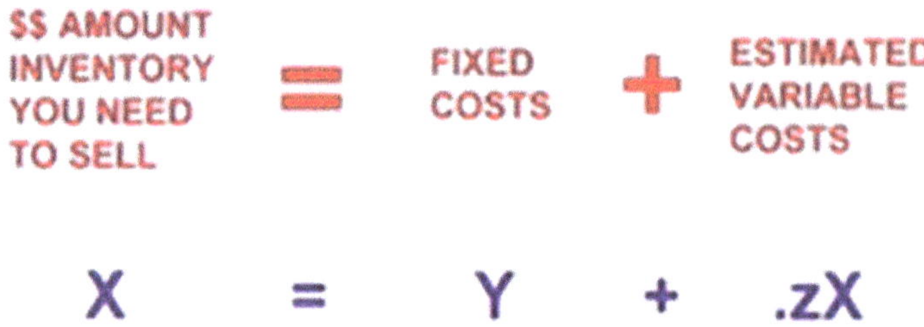

I want to introduce you to a quick and dirty breakeven analysis. I call this "Quick and Dirty" because we are using imperfect information. However, this imperfect information is good enough to help us make a decision whether a particular craft show is worth the risk.

Your breakeven point is where you have sold enough inventory to cover your costs. That is, *the total retail dollars you have taken in equals the sum of your fixed plus your variable costs.*

We use our quick and dirty breakeven analysis to answer the question:
How much inventory do I need to sell in order to breakeven?

Let's familiarize ourselves more with the components of the

formula, and then review the math.

FIXED COSTS

Fixed costs are costs that remain the same, regardless of how many items you sell at your craft fair.

Fixed costs include things like fees, travel, food, and staffing. Again, you have to lay out this money for fixed costs whether you made no money at all, or made a bucket full of money at your craft fair.

VARIABLE COSTS

Variable costs are costs that get incurred when each unit is sold.

Thus, variable costs fluctuate based on the number of units sold. If you sell very few pieces, your variable costs are low. If you sell a lot of pieces, your variable costs will be much higher. So, if a piece costs you $3.00 to make, and you sell 10 pieces, your variable costs are $30.00 (10 times $3.00); if you sell 100 pieces, your variable costs are $300.00 (100 times $3.00).

Variable costs include special packaging and displays, brochures and business cards handed out with each sale, credit card fees you are charged by the banks after each sale, and the cost of the parts used to make each piece that has sold.

We usually *estimate variable costs using some industry standards* about the percent of total retail price these costs are associated with. This saves a lot of time instead of diligently tracking the cost of each and every bead, stringing material, clasp, and other components used. For example, say you use a standard markup of 3x your costs. If the retail price were $12.00, then your costs would be estimated as $4.00 (thus, $12.00 divided by 3).

NOTES:

When we calculate the cost of inventory, we

differentiate between the cost of those pieces which we actually have sold from the cost of those pieces we did not sell. We need to do this for both tax accounting reasons as well as financial management best practices.

For purposes of developing a budget and calculating a breakeven analysis, to help us decide whether a particular craft show is worth the risk, we focus **only on the costs of inventory estimates based on what we sell**.

From an overall business standpoint, because you will want to *bring 4x the inventory* of what you predict will be sold, and these *additional out of pocket expenses associated with the pieces which would not be sold have not been included in our breakeven analysis*, you will need to be realistic, whether you can afford the show, or not.

So, if you sold $100.00 of jewelry, your costs of inventory sold would be $25.00. But, you would have had to have brought with you $400.00 of jewelry in order to sell $100.00. You would, in realty, have to lay out $100.00 to make that much inventory. You cannot, however, declare those other $75.00 of costs until you have sold the remaining $300.00 of jewelry at some future date.

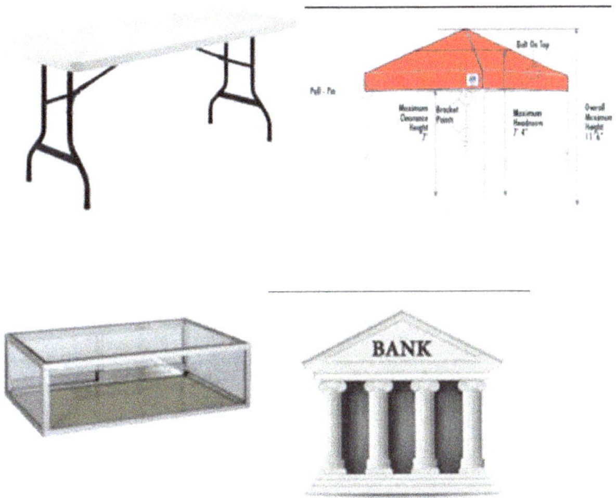

INVESTMENT COSTS

There are some additional costs you will incur which are also not included in our breakeven analysis. I'm going to call these *investment costs*.

Investment costs are things you pay for which have to last a very long time (much longer than 1 year), and which you will use at many, many craft shows.

These include *long term assets*, such as buying tables and chairs, a tent, and display cases.

These also include *long term liabilities*, such as paying down loans and credit card charges over a longer period of time.

We do not include these investment costs in our breakeven analyses.

ITEM	RATE	CALCULATED COST
FOOD / DRINK	$40.00/day	=$ 80.00
AUTO-TRAVEL	$110.00	=$110.00
LODGING	$65.00	=$ 65.00
FEES	$120.00	=$120.00
STAFFING	$80.00/day	=$160.00
TOTAL FIXED COSTS		=$535.00

ITEM	RATE	CALCULATED COST
SUPPLIES-DISPLAY	.05 x 1528.57	= $ 76.43
SUPPLIES-MARKETING	.12 x 1528.57	= $ 183.43
SUPPLIES-PACKING	.02 x 1528.57	= $ 30.57
CREDIT CARD FEES	.05 x 1528.57	= $ 76.43
CELL PHONE FEES	.01 x 1528.57	= $ 15.29
COSTS INVENTORY SOLD	.40 x 1528.57	= $ 611.42
TOTAL VARIABLE COSTS	.65 x 1528.57	= $ 993.57

FIXED AND VARIABLE COSTS LAID OUT WITHIN A BUDGET TABLE

Say you will be doing a 2-day craft show out of town, 200 miles away from home. And you will need to hire 1 person to help you. Let's look at our budget above for doing this particular craft show.

You have budgeted for your fixed and variable costs as

56

shown in the table above. I have plugged in some typical numbers into this budget table.

Our *fixed costs* are relatively easy to figure out.

ITEM	RATE	CALCULATED COST
FOOD / DRINK	$40.00/day	=$ 80.00
AUTO-TRAVEL	$110.00	=$110.00
LODGING	$65.00	=$ 65.00
FEES	$120.00	=$120.00
STAFFING	$80.00/day	=$160.00
TOTAL FIXED COSTS		=$535.00

Our *variable costs*, however, will have to be estimated. These variable costs are keyed off the retail prices you set for your jewelry. We will use some industry *percent of price standards*, as well as our breakeven analysis formula, to help us figure out the "TO BE CALCULATED" variable costs in our budget table. A simple Google search will pull up these industry standards. Looking at the table, for example, *supplies-marketing costs* are estimated as 12% (.12) of the *total expected retail sales (thus, revenue) ($1528.57).*

ITEM	RATE	CALCULATED COST
SUPPLIES-DISPLAY	.05 x 1528.57	= $ 76.43
SUPPLIES-MARKETING	.12 x 1528.57	= $ 183.43
SUPPLIES-PACKING	.02 x 1528.57	= $ 30.57
CREDIT CARD FEES	.05 x 1528.57	= $ 76.43
CELL PHONE FEES	.01 x 1528.57	= $ 15.29
COSTS INVENTORY SOLD	.40 x 1528.57	= $ 611.42
TOTAL VARIABLE COSTS	.65 x 1528.57	= $ 993.57

I have used 12% as the proportion of the total retail price that would be spent on marketing costs. These costs would include brochures, business cards, a post card mailing, some promotional ads, some effort to contact previous customers to let them know you will be at this craft show. The industry standard for marketing ranges between 5 and 15 per cent.

If you are getting started, you can use my numbers presented in this table. After you have done a few craft shows, you can begin to analyze your own sales and cost data, to develop what are called *multipliers* for each variable line-item category.

Again, our quick and dirty analysis is keyed off our retail prices.

I am assuming that you already know how to set fair and reasonable prices for your merchandise. If not, I would suggest reviewing my PRICING AND SELLING video

tutorial .
https://so-you-want-to-be-a-jewelry-
designer.teachable.com/p/pricing-and-selling-your-jewelry

FIXED COSTS		
Item	Projected Rate	Calculated Cost
FOOD AND DRINK	$40.00/DAY	= $80.00
AUTO-TRAVEL	$110.00	= $110.00
LODGING	$65.00	= $65.00
FEES	$120.00	= $120.00
STAFFING	$80.00/DAY	= $160.00
TOTAL FIXED COSTS		$535.00
VARIABLE COSTS		
SUPPLIES-DISPLAY	5% OF TOTAL INVENTORY SOLD (typically 1-5%)	TO BE CALCULATED
SUPPLIES-MARKETING	12% OF TOTAL INVENTORY SOLD (typically 5-15%)	TO BE CALCULATED
SUPPLIES-PACKING	2% OF TOTAL INVENTORY SOLD (typically 1-2%)	TO BE CALCULATED
CREDIT CARD CHARGES/FEES	5% OF TOTAL INVENTORY SOLD (typically 2-5%)	TO BE CALCULATED
TELEPHONE CHARGES/FEES	1% OF TOTAL INVENTORY SOLD (typically 1-2%)	TO BE CALCULATED
COSTS OF INVENTORY SOLD	40% OF TOTAL INVENTORY SOLD (typically between 35% - 60%)	TO BE CALCULATED
TOTAL VARIABLE COSTS	65% OF TOTAL INVENTORY SOLD (should total around 65% - 75% of total inventory sold)	TO BE CALCULATED
	TOTAL COSTS	TO BE CALCULATED

M	R
DISPLAY	.05 x
MARKETING	.12 x
PACKING	.02 x
RD FEES	.05 x
E FEES	.01 x
TORY SOLD	.40 x

BREAKEVEN FORMULA

$$\text{\$\$ AMOUNT INVENTORY YOU NEED TO SELL} = \text{FIXED COSTS} + \text{ESTIMATED VARIABLE COSTS}$$

$$X = Y + .zX$$

OUR BREAKEVEN FORMULA HAS 3 VARIABLES:

X

Y

and

.zX

X stands for the amount of inventory we will need to sell to breakeven. This will, in effect, be the total of all retail prices of our merchandise we need to sell, that is, it will be our total revenue.

Y is the total of all our fixed costs.

.zX is our last variable. This is our estimate of the total variable costs. We estimate total variable costs as a *percent* of the total of all retail prices of merchandise sold. That is, as a *percent of revenue*.

Look back at our developing budget table.

ITEM	RATE	CALCULATED COST
FOOD / DRINK	$40.00/day	=$ 80.00
AUTO-TRAVEL	$110.00	=$110.00
LODGING	$65.00	=$ 65.00
FEES	$120.00	=$120.00
STAFFING	$80.00/day	=$160.00
TOTAL FIXED COSTS		=$535.00

ITEM	RATE	CALCULATED COST
SUPPLIES-DISPLAY	.05 x 1528.57	= $ 76.43
SUPPLIES-MARKETING	.12 x 1528.57	= $ 183.43
SUPPLIES-PACKING	.02 x 1528.57	= $ 30.57
CREDIT CARD FEES	.05 x 1528.57	= $ 76.43
CELL PHONE FEES	.01 x 1528.57	= $ 15.29
COSTS INVENTORY SOLD	.40 x 1528.57	= $ 611.42
TOTAL VARIABLE COSTS	.65 x 1528.57	= $ 993.57

Y, WHICH IS OUR FIXED COSTS TOTAL = 535.00

.z IS THAT PERCENT OF REVENUE REPRESENTING TOTAL VARIABLE COSTS.

.z= .65 *(.65 IS SUM OF OUR MULTIPLERS IN OUR BUDGET TABLE*
.05+.12+.02+.05+.01+.40)

So, in this case study, we expect our variable costs to total 65% of our total expected revenue.

SOLVE FOR X

Next, using our breakeven formula, we solve for X.

To solve for X, we need to re-organize our formula so that the X variable,
which occurs twice in our formula, is *all put on one side of the equation.*

THIS IS HOW WE SOLVE THIS FORMULA:

We start with:

$$X = 535.00 + .65X$$

We move the .65X to the left side, by subtracting it from both sides. This, in effect, zero's out the .65X on the right side.

$$X - .65X = 535.00$$

We combine both X variables, which, in effect, let's us subtract on the right side the .65X from 1X, leaving us with .35X. When we write X, this is the same as writing 1 times X, or 1X.

$$.35X = 535.00$$

We solve for X. We divide both sides of the equation by .35. This leaves 1X on the left side.

$$X = 535/.35$$

And, we get our Breakeven Point of $1528.57! Given this craft show scenario, we will need to sell $1528.57 of merchandise (thus, our total revenue) to breakeven. That is because we have $535.00 of fixed costs and $993.57 of estimated variable costs. This adds up to a total of $1528.57 in costs.

$$X = 1528.57$$

Let's look at our variable costs calculations:

VARIABLE COSTS		
SUPPLIES-DISPLAY	5% OF TOTAL INVENTORY SOLD	=$76.43
SUPPLIES-MARKETING	12% OF TOTAL INVENTORY SOLD	=$183.43
SUPPLIES-PACKING	2% OF TOTAL INVENTORY SOLD	=$30.57
CREDIT CARD CHARGES/FEES	5% OF TOTAL INVENTORY SOLD	=$76.43
TELEPHONE CHARGES/FEES	1% OF TOTAL INVENTORY SOLD	=$15.29
COSTS OF INVENTORY SOLD	40% OF TOTAL INVENTORY SOLD	=$611.42
TOTAL VARIABLE COSTS	65% OF TOTAL INVENTORY SOLD	$993.57
	TOTAL COSTS	$1528.57

So, to break even, we would need to sell a retail total of $1528.57 of merchandise at our 2-day show. To sell that much inventory, we would need to bring about 4 times that much, or $6,000.00 of inventory with us.

**Let's review this breakeven formula application
again, in English.**

For those of you who haven't had algebra, or are
somewhat math-phobic, I want to go over the mathematical
analysis in more English terms. It is important to
understand the concepts, and to understand how to do the
math.

First, we have the breakeven formula itself.
Basically, it says:

100% of Breakeven revenue
Equals
The Total of all our costs.

Some of these costs are *fixed*, meaning we have to pay
for them, whether we make any money or not.

Some of these costs are *variable*, meaning we only
incur these costs when we sell something. The amount of
variable costs "Varies" based on how much we sell.

We are trying to figure out how much we need to sell in
order to breakeven. We can easily figure out our fixed costs.
We estimate our variable costs as a percent of revenues.

In this particular example,

Our fixed costs were $535.00. So, Y = $535.00
We estimated our variable costs as 65% of revenues. So our variable costs = .65 times X.

This is all the information we need to do the algebra in the formula and figure out our breakeven revenue=costs point, which we have called "X".

We begin to re-state the formula as:
100% of revenue equals $535.00 + 65% of revenue.

So, we continue to play with the formula so that we get: Total Breakeven Revenues on one side of the equals sign, and everything else on the other side.

We have to do this is a few steps.

We re-write the formula again:
100% of revenue minus 65% of revenues equals $535.00.

And we simplify this a little by writing the formula as:
100% minus 65% times revenues = $535.00

And simplifying the formula even more, we subtract 65% from 100% and get 35%,

 and the formula reads:
35% times revenues = $535.00

Since we want to end up with 100% of revenues on one side of the equation,
and the dollar amount that this 100% equals on the other side, we have to do one more math step.

To change .35X to 1X, we have to divide it by .35.

Mathematically, if we do something to one side of the equation, we have to do it to the other side, as well.

That's how we get:
100% of revenues = $535.00 divided by 35%.

And the answer is that our breakeven revenue, where our sales equals our costs, is
$1528.57

So, to breakeven, we would need to sell a retail total of $1528.57 of merchandise at our 2-day show. To sell that much inventory, we would need to bring about 4x that much, or $6,000.00 of inventory with us.

While we do not include the costs of this additional inventory, and which we assumed would not sell, we still need to anticipate in our realistic goal setting process, the financial impact of all this.

Let's update our budget table for this 2-day craft show example:

FIXED COSTS		
FOOD AND DRINK	$40.00/DAY	= $80.00
AUTO-TRAVEL	$110.00	= $110.00
LODGING	$65.00	= $65.00
FEES	$120.00	= $120.00
STAFFING	$80.00/DAY	= $160.00
TOTAL FIXED COSTS		$535.00
VARIABLE COSTS		
SUPPLIES-DISPLAY	5% OF TOTAL INVENTORY SOLD	=$76.43
SUPPLIES-MARKETING	12% OF TOTAL INVENTORY SOLD	=$183.43
SUPPLIES-PACKING	2% OF TOTAL INVENTORY SOLD	=$30.57
CREDIT CARD CHARGES/FEES	5% OF TOTAL INVENTORY SOLD	=$76.43
TELEPHONE CHARGES/FEES	1% OF TOTAL INVENTORY SOLD	=$15.29
COSTS OF INVENTORY SOLD	40% OF TOTAL INVENTORY SOLD	=$611.42
TOTAL VARIABLE COSTS	65% OF TOTAL INVENTORY SOLD	$993.57
	TOTAL COSTS	$1528.57

ONE MORE EXAMPLE

Now, let's review our breakeven analysis with another example.

Say you are doing a 1-day craft show, close to home, low fees, you bring your own tables, and you don't need electricity, and don't need extra staffing. Also, you don't plan on doing a lot of marketing.

Exercise: Breakeven Analysis

1 Day Craft Show

Close To Home

Low Fees

Bring own tables, do not need electricity, do not need extra staffing, do not plan on doing a lot of extra marketing.

1.   SET UP YOUR BUDGET_(list fixed costs; list multipliers for variable costs)

First, you begin to set up a Budget.

Here we have fixed costs equal to $70.00.

Our variable costs we estimate to be 54% of our total revenues.

FIXED COSTS		
Item	Projected Rate Per Day	Calculated Cost
FOOD AND DRINK		
AUTO-TRAVEL		
LODGING		
FEES		
STAFFING		
TOTAL FIXED COSTS		
VARIABLE COSTS		
SUPPLIES-DISPLAY	___% OF TOTAL INVENTORY SOLD (typically 1-5%)	TO BE CALCULATED
SUPPLIES-MARKETING	___% OF TOTAL INVENTORY SOLD (typically 5-15%)	TO BE CALCULATED
SUPPLIES-PACKING	___% OF TOTAL INVENTORY SOLD (typically 1-2%)	TO BE CALCULATED
CREDIT CARD CHARGES/FEES	___% OF TOTAL INVENTORY SOLD (typically 2-5%)	TO BE CALCULATED
TELEPHONE CHARGES/FEES	___% OF TOTAL INVENTORY SOLD (typically 1-2%)	TO BE CALCULATED
COSTS OF INVENTORY SOLD	___% OF TOTAL INVENTORY SOLD (typically between 35% - 60%; think about how much you mark up your jewelry to price it)	TO BE CALCULATED
TOTAL VARIABLE COSTS	___% OF TOTAL INVENTORY SOLD (should total around 65% - 75% of total inventory sold)	TO BE CALCULATED
	TOTAL COSTS	Fixed + Variable Costs

Next, we calculate our breakeven point, using our quick and dirty formula.

BREAKEVEN ANALYSIS: _(What is the value of "X"?)

$$X = Y + .zX$$

X   INVENTORY NEEDED TO BREAK EVEN (TOTAL RETAIL VALUE)

Y   FIXED COSTS TOTAL

.z   PERCENT OF REVENUE REPRESENTING TOTAL VARIABLE COSTS

INVENTORY WE NEED TO BRING WITH US:

$$4 * X = \underline{\hspace{3cm}}$$

Where, Y=70 and .z=.54
and the formula leads us to dividing 70 by .46, to get
$152.17

We see our breakeven point is $152.17. And using our rule of thumb about how much inventory to bring, we need to bring *4 x $152.17*, or about $600.00 of inventory.

The Next Question To Ask Ourselves:
How Much Profit Do You Want To Make?

How much more money do you want to make above and beyond your breakeven point?

You don't just want to breakeven. You want to make a profit. At our breakeven point, we have covered both our fixed costs and our variable costs. Our fixed costs are now all paid for.

As we bring in more addition revenues, we will have more variable but no more fixed costs to cover. Our additional revenues will only be based on how much more we sell, after subtracting our variable costs.

Example 1 above: In our first example, our breakeven point was $1528.57.

In this example, 65 cents of each dollar in price that was earned was spent on variable costs, and 35 cents on each dollar earned was spent on fixed costs.

As we go beyond our breakeven point, and become profitable, again in this example, we would be spending only 65 cents out of each additional revenue dollar for variable costs.

We would have no more fixed costs.

If we had sold one more dollar, we would have had 35 cents remaining. We could have used that remaining 35 cents out of each dollar of additional revenue to pay for some of our investment costs, as well as pay ourselves something.

Profit Goal

How much of a profit goal you want to set is your personal choice. However, I like to tell students that breaking even at the show itself is OK, if you also have strategies in place to generate follow-up sales, either through repeat sales between shows, or repeat sales at the next show.

Think About Reinvestment

A*s **we go beyond our breakeven point, and become profitable,** we could have used that remaining 35 cents out of each dollar of additional revenue to pay for some of our investment costs, as well as pay ourselves something.

Investment costs are things you pay for which either have to last a very long time, and which you will use at many, many craft shows, or which involve expanding your core jewelry making supplies inventory beyond what you need to replace the parts represented by the items sold.

These include "long term assets", such as buying tables and chairs, a tent, and display cases. These also include "long term liabilities", such as paying down loans and credit card charges.

We *do not include* these investment costs in our break-even analyses.

Good selling face vs. bored selling face

WHAT DID THEY NEED
TO PREPARE THEMSELVES

TO *SELL?*

Selecting and doing craft shows requires research and planning. And it requires an ability to keep up a good "Retail Personality" while standing on your feet for long hours, sometimes when it's too hot or too cold or too windy and dusty.

Selling Jewelry requires a different mind-set than *Creating Jewelry.* If you don't have the personality for Selling, bring a friend with you who does.

WHAT AMOUNT OF REPEAT BUSINESS AND FOLLOW-UP SALES SHOULD YOU LOOK FOR?

A good goal to set is to generate repeat business equal to 25%.

So, if you have 10 sales at the show, your goal would be to get 3 repeat sales. These could occur when the customer contacts you between shows. These could also occur at the next show you do, when the customer buys from you again. These could occur when a customer spreads *word-of-mouth*, and influences someone else to buy something from you.

You will make a might higher profit and experience better long-term outcomes, through repeat business. With repeat business, you can considerably lower your variable costs, particularly those associated with marketing. Because of this, that 2nd or follow-up sale is often more important than that 1st sale at the show.

Lesson 4 was to set Realistic Goals.

It is OK to start small. To start locally. To gradually take on bigger and bigger shows, while you are establishing your reputation and building a following.

You obviously want to keep your expenses to a minimum, and there can be some steep up-front costs, such as creating a sufficient inventory.

Starting small gives you a chance to test out your ideas about costs, whether you like doing craft shows, whether there is a good fit between your merchandise and the shows, and whether there is a good fit between your personality and doing craft shows.

When you start, you might be able to share booth space with another friend who has a business, and share some of those other fixed costs, like travel and fees.

Do your homework when selecting craft shows which fit well with your goals and your budget. Figure out your breakeven point, and how much inventory you need to bring to make a profit.

As Roland and Rolanda should have done.

LESSON 5:
Get Those Applications In Early

John Jacob thought he could set up anywhere and anytime. So he missed the April 30th deadline for the Red Hills Fair. And he sent in an incomplete application without the required pictures to Napa Sweets Festival. And he didn't take seriously the fact that Naples Symphony Days was a juried competition. And he couldn't understand how adding one more jewelry vendor to the Rocky Mountain Showroom would make much of a difference.

He had calculated that he needed to do 4 shows a year to make a living. But for several years now, although he had applied to at least 12 shows each year, he rarely was approved for more than 2.

THE APPLICATION

1. PREPARE A GENERIC APPLICATION

2. UNDERSTAND THE JURIED SELECTION PROCESS

3. SUBMIT APPLICATIONS AND FOLLOW-UP ON THEM

4. SCHEDULE YOURSELF FOR THE YEAR

Art League Of Marco Island
Fine Craft Festival 2013

Date of Show: March 16th & 17th, 2013
Setup Time : 6:30AM - 9:30AM
Place: 1010 Winterberry Dr, Marco Island, FL 34145

Date Of Application: ____

Applicant Name: ____

Business Address: ____

Business / Home Phone: ____

Email Address: ____

License Plate #: ____

(Deadline for applications: When Full)
PLEASE ENCLOSE 3 PHOTOS OF YOUR CRAFTS AND ONE OF YOUR BOOTH
(Please enclose a self-addressed, stamped envelope)
(Your acceptance will be sent to you by mail)

PLEASE DESCRIBE YOUR CRAFT:

____

____

____

Consider my application for:
BOOTH FEE: $175.00 PLUS TAX: $10.50 PLUS APPLICATION FEE: $10.00
No. of spaces _________ 10 x 10 @ $195.50

Make checks payable to: Pam Patullo
Directors reserve the right to accept or deny applications.
ALL ITEMS MUST BE HANDMADE
Any questions call Pam Patullo at: 732-682-3230 or 732-223-3710

Return completed applications to:

Pam Patullo
966 Sundrop Ct
Marco Island, FL 34145

The undersigned agrees to abide by all regulations set forth by the promoter, Pam Patullo. Art League Of Marco Island or any of their workers shall not be held liable for property damage or personal injury to exhibitors, its agents or employees regardless of how such injury or damage may have occurred. Promoter reserves the right to accept or reject any exhibitor and shall have the right to make rules and regulations for the show that it deems proper and necessary

Signature: ____

Sample Application Form

1. PREPARE A GENERIC APPLICATION

Some organizations have a formal, printed application form to fill out. More and more, however, organizations are using online application services.

I suggest creating a generic application form, from which you can cut and paste into these printed or online application forms.

Application/Acceptance Process

Read ALL THE FINE PRINT.
COMPLETE the Application forms COMPLETELY.
Be sure to meet all DEADLINES.
Include your CHECK/MONEY ORDER for all required PREPAYMENTS and DEPOSITS.

If you need special arrangements, be sure to negotiate these up front. Do you need electricity or special lighting or special access? Do you prefer to have a particular location or table arrangement? Will your displays conform to the show's expectations, requirements and limitations? If you will be doing demonstrations, will all your equipment and tools meet show requirements or not? Do you need to be on a corner?

Is this a juried show?
Are there additional costs besides the booth rental, such as required advertising expenses, parking fees, electricity fees, tables and chairs, insurance requirements, and the like? Are there are restrictions as to the type of merchandise allowed, such as a requirement that all merchandise be hand-crafted by the artist.

Are promotional materials such as brochures or postcards provided to exhibitors?

Be sure to find out ahead of time,

- What times you have to be ready and fully set up in your booth
- What time you have to wait until before you can take down your booth
- How early you can begin to set up your booth

Company Info
    SUNSHINE JEWELRY
    718 Thompson Lane, Ste 123, Nashville, TN 37204
    615-292-0610
    bebe@sunshinejewelry.org
    License Plate: 631-132 TN
    Resale #: 101-555 TN
Merchandise Sold
    Jewelry
Hand made?
    Everything is hand made
Price Range
    $5.00 - $250.00
Describe Your Craft
    Bead strung, wire-worked, bead-woven pieces
Artist Statement
    Experience, Approach and Techniques, Current Activity,
    Awards, Publications
Booth Size Requirements
    10'x10' space
Additional Services Needed
    Electricity, 3x6' table rental
Attach 5 photos of merchandise
Attach 3 photos of booth and display
Special preferences
    None
Credit Card Number
    Visa, -3543, 01/11, 123

Say, This Was Your Company

On the Application, they may ask you for these types of
information:

     1. Company information, address, phone, email,

contact phone, onsite-contact phone, website, license plate #, re-sale or tax number and state which issued it

2. Type of merchandise to be sold

3. Hand-made?

4. High and low price range of merchandise

5. Describe your craft (techniques, materials, designs)

6. Artist Statement (about 150-250 words)

7. Booth size requirements (will you need more than one 10'x10' booth space?)

8. Requirements for additional services, such as electricity, table and chair rental, tent

9. 5 photos of your crafts (be sure your photos are sharp and attractive, as if they were publishing in a book. No dark photos. .jpg or .tif)

10. With photos, you might need slides, or you might need .jpg images that are 72-96 dpi, or you might need hi-resolution .jpg images which are 300 or 600 dpi. Use 16-bit color. Be prepared with each of these.

11. 3 photos of your booth set-up (They want visually appealing, customer enticing, user friendly booth set-ups, again, no dark photos.)

12. List of special preferences, such as "corner

booth, if available".

13. Credit card number, expiration date, security code number, billing address (They will probably want this number to keep on file).

2. UNDERSTAND THE JURIED SELECTION PROCESS

At this point, you have selected shows which you feel are a good fit with your business.

Now, determine if you are eligible for them. Do they put any limitations on who can and cannot apply? Do they require that your creative work be juried?

Most craft shows make simple acceptance decisions based on

- *Submitting an application form, and*
- *Paying the fee*

Some may restrict the number of jewelry vendors they accept, because they want a balance of types of merchandise, and often, too many jewelry vendors apply.

Other shows want to maintain some level of merchandise quality standards. They subject the applicant to a more intensive jury-review process.

The jury process is probably what you would expect. Usually a few people review all the application and score them against a set of criteria. They choose the ones which score the highest.

Some typical criteria they use:

- Products considered best for the show

- Aesthetics and visual appeal

- Functionality

- Creativity

- Originality

- Technique

- Marketability

- Quality of work

- Booth design

They want to end up with vendors whose wares will sell, where there won't be much duplication, and whose presence and set-up is exciting for the people who attend the show.

Your short write-up and submitted photographs need to make your case.

***WHAT DOES IT MEAN
WHEN A JUROR SAYS "NO!"?***

Most rejections are based on the limited number of openings, particularly for jewelry vendors.

Another major reason for rejections is the poor quality of photos submitted. Look at your photos. Share them with some friends. Judge them according to the previously discussed judging criteria. How well do they make your case? Are they clear, focused, bright?

3. SUBMIT APPLICATIONS
AND FOLLOW-UP ON THEM

You have created your list of possible shows, based on your sense of fit, the goals you have set for yourself, and your budget, given the costs involved. You have determined whether you are eligible for them.

Decide about how many shows you want to do a year. Select 5-10 more shows in addition to the number you want to do.

Another rule of thumb is to select 3 events to apply to for each weekend you want to work. If you want to work 4 weekends, then apply to 12 events.

Get their application forms, and review the rules and application deadlines.

READ ALL THE RULES !!!

Determine how long their review processes are, and figure out when you should know whether you have been accepted.

Call or email each one, and verify that all the information you have – dates, fees, application requirements, deadlines – are true. Things change. Things get printed wrong.

***NOTE: Things change. Things get printed wrong.*

4. SCHEDULE YOURSELF FOR THE YEAR

Organization is critical here.

Get a good 3-year calendar. Map out every date. Every Application deadline. Every application acceptance notification. Every deadline for notifying them, confirming your acceptance, and submitting any up-front fees. Every show date, including set-up and break-down dates and times.

Remember, for many craft shows, you will be applying 6-12 months ahead of time.

It takes a lot of coordinated effort to keep everything on track. You might set up a spread-sheet or data-base. I use a calendar app that links with my email program. I set up automatic reminders, so they pop up when I need to take action.

After you send in your fees, follow-up in 2 weeks to be sure they received your application and payment.

5. BEFORE SAYING YES!...

Re-review your

- Fit with the show

- Break-even analysis

- Calendar schedule

- The money needed up front

And, ...

- Whether there are any cancellation penalties or

rules

- What kinds of local and state licenses, certificates and permits you will need

- If the show promoters assist you in obtaining temporary ones for the duration of the show

LESSON 6:
Promote, Promote, Promote

You need to actively promote yourself, both before and after the show.

Do not rely on the show promoters to do all the marketing.

January | February | March

April | May | June

July | August | September

October | November | December

About 2-4 weeks before the show:

a. Contact your existing customers (email, mail, social network sites)

b. Promote your message to potential customers. Leave flyers and brochures at relevant businesses or organizations. Post messages on social network sites. Post messages on your own website or blog. Get listed on community calendars. Tell people you interact with.

In your promotions, be sure you have all the details listed correctly. In a short, catchy phrase or sentence, tell why this event would be of particular interest to them. You might offer special discounts, if they present your card or email notice.

c. Be sure you are going to look presentable. If you need a hair-cut, get it. Be sure you have all the clothes you need. Check your supply of business cards, brochures, other promotional materials. Practice

94

saying your selling points. Be strategic about which pieces of jewelry you are going to wear at the show.

AT THE SHOW:

Have your business cards, and any brochures, if you have them, out for the taking. It helps if your business cards have an image of your jewelry on them to help people remember you.

Have a book or sign-up sheet where people can list their names, mailing and emailing addresses.

AFTER THE SHOW:

Update your customer database. Stay in touch with your new customers, such as with a follow-up mailing or emailing.

Direct your new customers to your website, or other ways of contacting you and seeing your pieces which are for sale.

LESSON 7:
Set Up For Success

Imogene McAllsiter Rosenstein. Remember she had no plan or strategy for choosing shows. And, guess what, she had no plan or strategy for setting up at shows, either.

Imogene, bless her heart, loved plaids. She would set up a table, and cover it with a dark, plaid cloth, and lay her jewelry onto the cloth. She liked to push her table up to the front of the booth, and sit in a chair behind it. Her boxes of supplies and inventory were stacked up against the back of her booth, no effort to disguise or hide them.

YOUR BOOTH IS YOUR SHOP

Your booth should be cohesive, visually interesting and functional.

You do not want your booth to be disorganized, dis-inviting, intimidating.

Setting up for success means having a good understanding of...

1. Booth Design
2. Lay-Out, Table Set Up, Traffic Flow
3. Merchandise display
4. Signage
5. Loading and Un-Loading

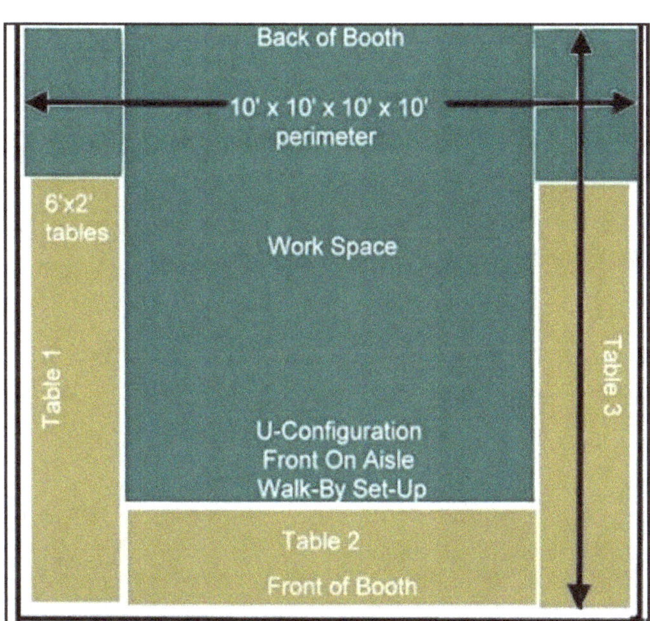

Back of Booth
10' x 10' x 10' x 10' perimeter
6'x2' tables
Work Space
Table 1
Table 3
U-Configuration
Front On Aisle
Walk-By Set-Up
Table 2
Front of Booth

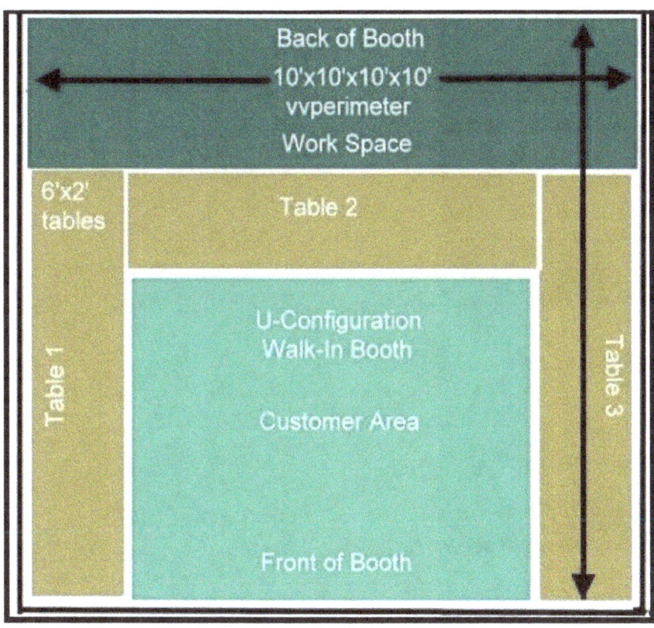

Back of Booth
10'x10'x10'x10' vvperimeter
Work Space
6'x2' tables
Table 2
Table 1
Table 3
U-Configuration
Walk-In Booth
Customer Area
Front of Booth

1. BOOTH DESIGN

A typical booth space is 10' x 10'. Plan to use this space wisely.

A 10'x10' booth will hold three 6-foot tables in a U-configuration.

Verify with the show promoters what your "foot-print" is. This might include additional space around or in front of your 10x10 foot space. If so, take advantage of that fact.

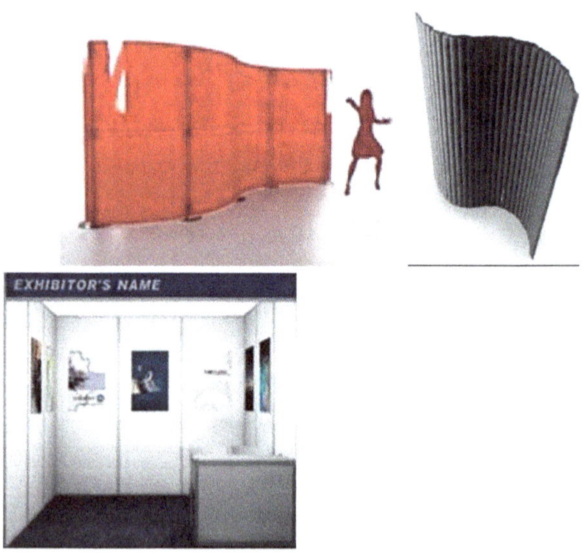

 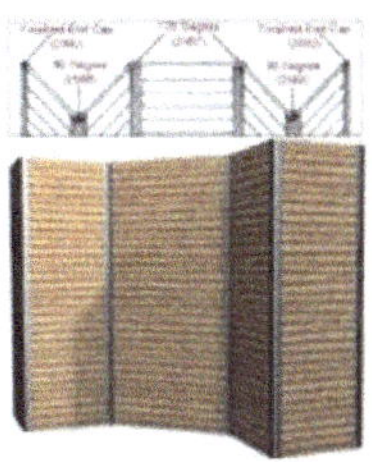

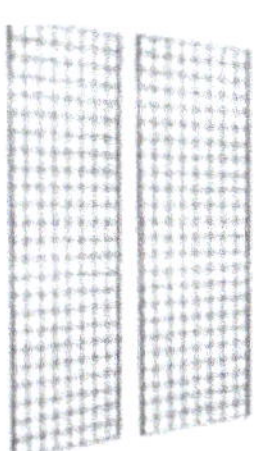

PARTITIONS

First, will this space be enclosed in some way – walls, partitions, inside a tent?

Do you want to have walls? Do the walls need to be fabric, wood, wire grids or chicken wire? What are you going to do with the walls? Can things be hung? How do these walls affect the visibility of your booth space and your inventory?

As best as I can, I like to use materials and furnishings which will not diminish the visibility of my booth, and which can do double-time. I often use window shutters or wire grids for walls and racks, so that I can hang things from them. The containers I use to tote my inventory and supplies get used for displays, or as support columns for displays.

The containers I use to tote my inventory and supplies get used for displays, or as support columns for displays.

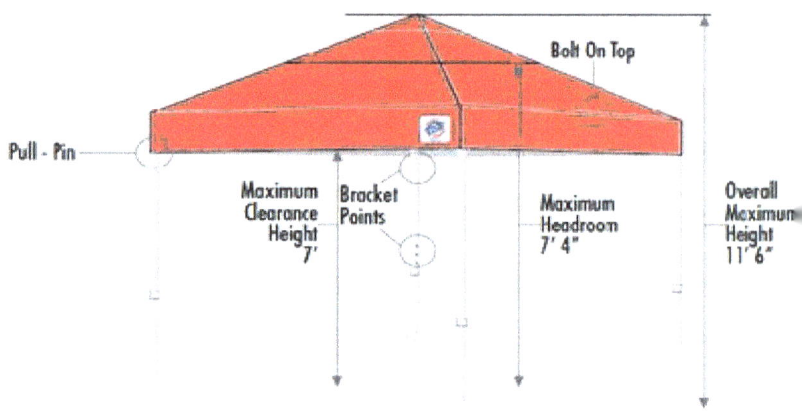

TENT

If you need a tent, some shows provide them or rent

them. Some shows have detailed requirements for what tents should look like. Sometimes they want all tents to be white. You can find online sources for buying tents. EZ-UP Brand (https://www.ezup.com) is one of them.

You want a tent where you can roll the walls up and down. Be sure you have tent weights, to deal with windy weather. Sometimes, if the air is hot and humid, and the tent walls are down, the air in your booth becomes stale and heavy. Don't let this happen.

Second, if you are to be provided with tables, how many and of what size will they be?

I find 6' by 2' tables to be especially easy to maneuver and manage.

For each table, I have cut up PVC pipe to stick the legs of my tables in. This allows me to raise the height of the tables about 6-9", so customers do not have to bend down so far to view the inventory. You will probably want to have a few sets of PVC pipe at different lengths, because the design/positioning of legs on various table models will differ.

I do not like tables flush with the aisle. In some settings, this is your only choice. But this makes it uncomfortable for people to stand there and look at your stuff. They are too concerned they may block someone in the aisle. If possible, move the tables inward 6-12" so you get them to feel like they have stepped into your booth.

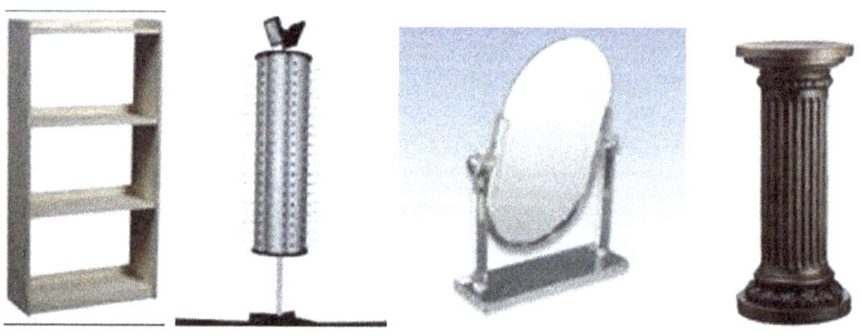

ADDITIONAL FURNISHINGS

Third, what kinds of additional furnishings will you need to bring?

Do things need to go on shelves? Is there room for some kind of rack? Do you want to put a rung on the floor, or in front of your booth? Do you want to bring box fans (or space heaters)? What will you use to store things you need access to during the show?

Bring a mirror for your customers.

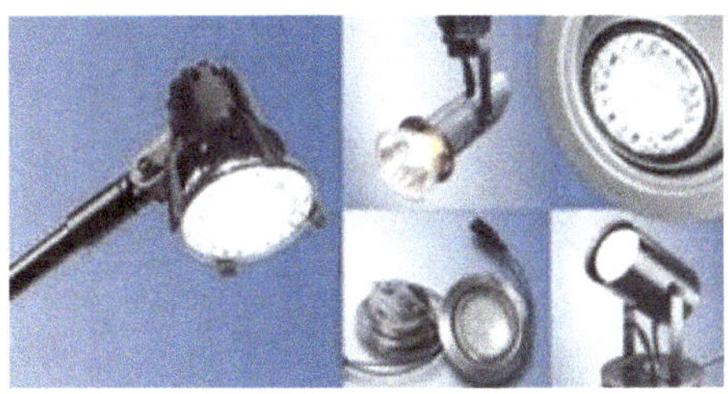

LIGHTING

Fourth, what is your lighting plan, and towards this end, will you have access to electricity?

Having lighting makes a big difference in your sales results. Bright LED lights, at 4100K to 5500K, sometimes labeled as "DAYLIGHT", are best. This Kelvin measure will give you a bluish white light.

Bring power strips and long extension cords. There may be electricity, but the source of this power may be located far from your booth. If there is no electricity, you can purchase battery operated or solar powered (if outside) LED lights.

FLOOR PLANS

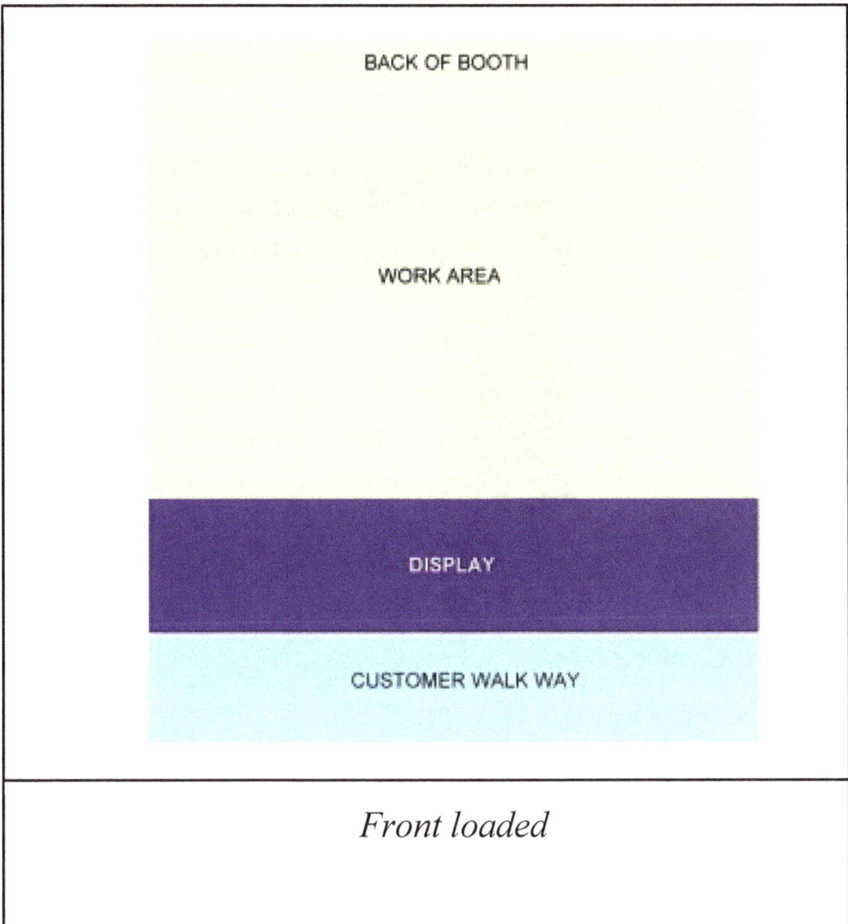

Front loaded

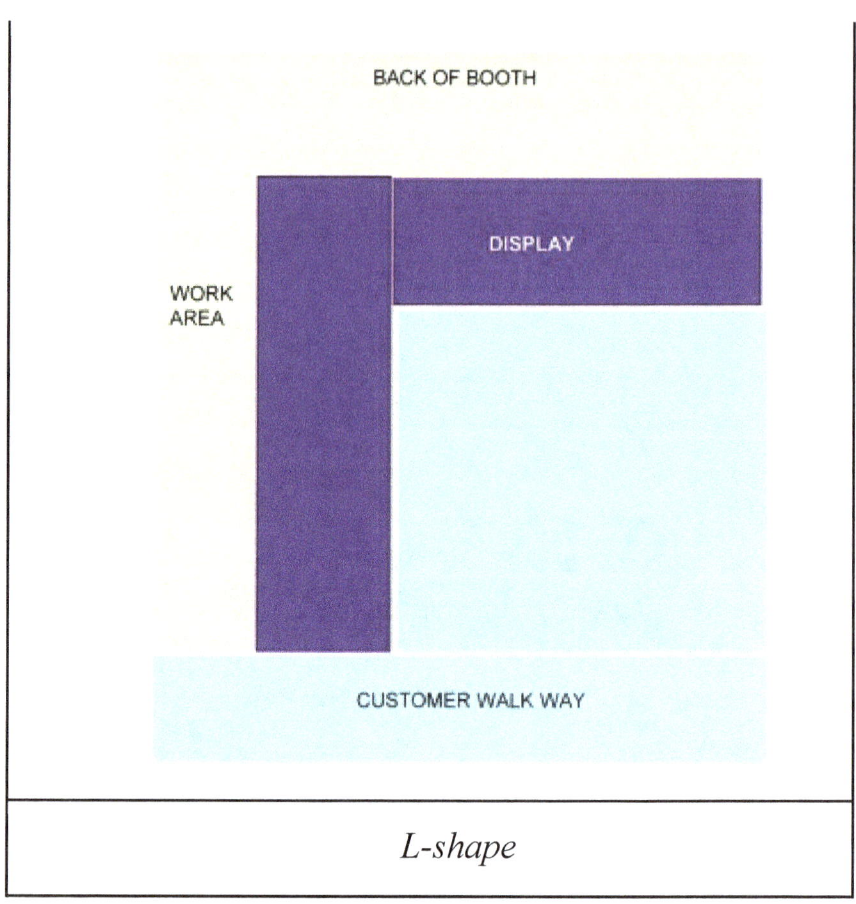

L-shape

108

BACK OF BOOTH
WORK AREA
WORK AREA
DISPLAY AREA
CUSTOMER WALK WAY

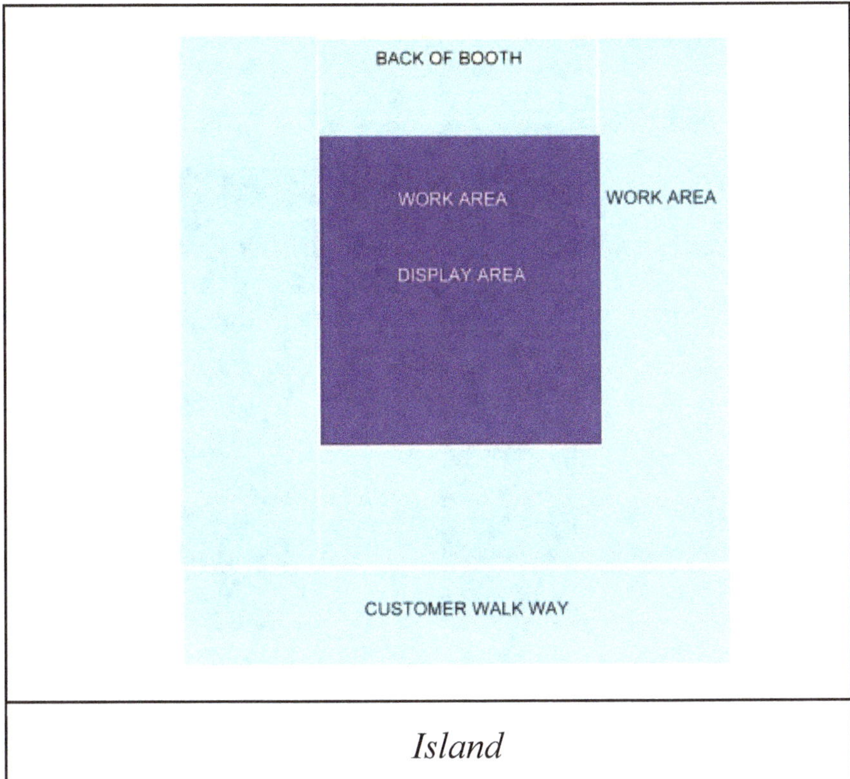

Island

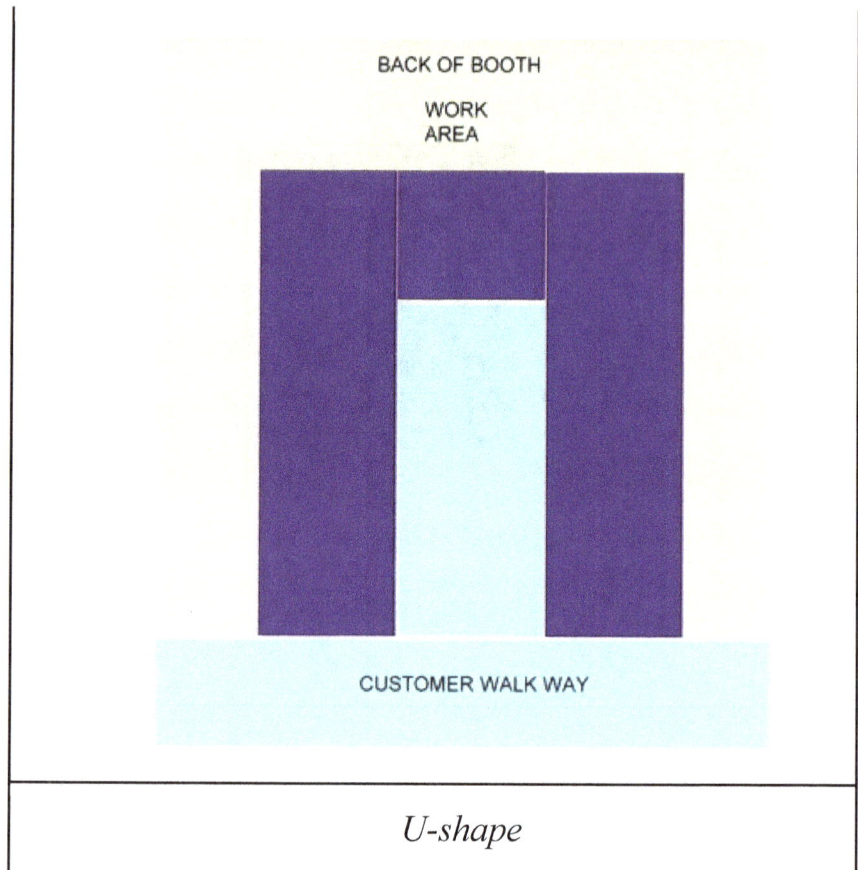

U-shape

FLOOR PLANS: L-SHAPE, U-SHAPE, FRONT-LOAD, ISLAND

Fifth, given the space, what is the optimum floor plan

110

for your booth?

If possible, I prefer to allow my customers to walk into part of my booth. Towards this end, again if possible, I like to set the tables up either in an "L-SHAPE" or a "U-SHAPE".

People don't like to stand in a place where they feel someone might brush against their behind while walking by.

SETTING THINGS UP

Last, practice, practice, practice.

Practice setting everything up. Practice packing your things, transporting your things, and un-packing your things. If you will be using a tent, practice setting this up.

Can you do all this by yourself? Given the distance between where you will have to park, and where your booth is, can you manage transporting all your stuff this distance?

Do you need a handtrucks or a flatbed on wheels?

What tools will you need? (hammer, screwdriver, wrench, pliers, and the like; screws, nails, tape, duct tape)

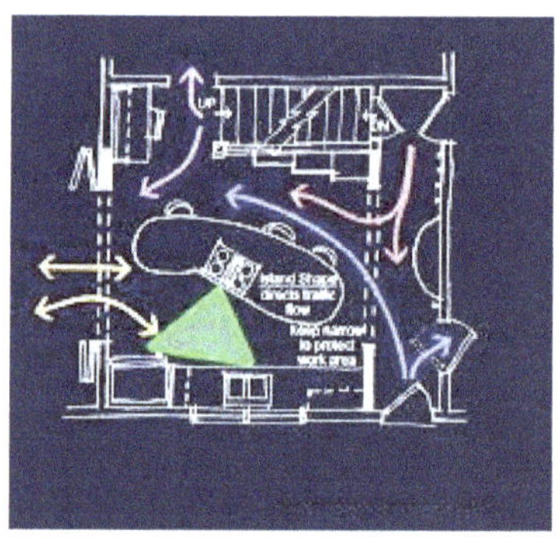

Traffic Flow

2. LAY-OUT, TABLE SET UP, TRAFFIC FLOW

Let's talk more specifically about lay-out and table set up.

CAN CUSTOMERS...

- ***ENTER AND EXIT EASILY***

- ***SHOP EASILY***

- ***PAY EASILY***

- ***NOT FEEL TRAPPED, WHEN A LOT OF PEOPLE ARE IN YOUR BOOTH***

Anticipate the traffic flow, both in front of your booth, as well as inside your booth, if you can set up to allow people to come inside.

Remember: Your space and customer flow go beyond the boundaries of your table.

Remember: Visualize how traffic will flow to and from each of your neighbors.

As shoppers walk by your booth, how much of it can they see? Are there things, and enough things, to catch their eye, and entice them to stop and look?

Be sure the décor of your booth coordinates well with the jewelry you are selling. It must coordinate with the show, as well. You don't want beach décor at a Christmas holiday show.

Prevent the *Scratched Tush Syndrome*. Customers avoid standing where they fear someone will brush against their back-sides.

PAYMENT STATION

Set up a payment station where customers can make their purchases out of the way of other shoppers, but where you can still keep an eye on things.

At your payment station, you will need to accept payment and make change, accept credit cards, and you will need to be able to write some kind of customer receipt. You may need to wrap up or package an item.

You do not want anyone but yourself (and staff) to have easy, grab-able access to your money or equipment.

SOME ADDITIONAL QUICK POINTERS:

- Cover your tables with fabric

- Don't use dark colors. These bring the mood down, and often don't enhance your jewelry in these very open settings

- Choose colors which add to your product, but do not compete with them

- Customers like to use all their sense when they shop: SEE, TOUCH, THINK and also SMELL and TASTE

- Subtly use props and mirrors to help the customer visualize how the product might be used or worn

- I like to make my booth feel homey.

- I like to have rugs inside as well as in front of my booth

- I like to have chairs or a bench near the front of my booth, to attract people to sit and linger, and so it always looks like people are looking at my booth

- In hot weather, I like to have a fan circulating air where the customers are standing, not just me. If I can provide any kind of shade (from a tent overhang, a tree, whatever), that's an added plus.

- In cold weather, I have a heater going.

- In rainy weather, I have a place people can lay down or store their umbrellas while they shop.

- No garbage should be visible

- Everything should be stored and neat

- Have enough signage to get people's attention, and educate them about your products

- Display your prices clearly

ANTICIPATE THE WEATHER

IS IT...

- HOT AND HUMID

- COLD

- RAINY OR STORMY

- WINDY

- DUSTY

Have drop cloths to protect your merchandise and displays.

I keep large pieces of cardboard that I can lay on wet ground, when my booth is outside. Sometimes I take a bale or two of straw that I purchased at the local hardware store or garden center, to cover wet ground.

I have plenty of cleaning aids, to keep the merchandise looking fresh and saleable all during the show.

I wear layers of clothing. I bring sunglasses, gloves, hats, a battery-powered hand-held fan, whatever it takes to keep me perky, happy and comfortable.

3. MERCHANDISE DISPLAY

As we have discovered already, Imogene McAllister Rosenstein had lots of things to learn about doing craft shows. Her displays of jewelry were very cluttered. Very flat looking. Never caught the attention of anyone's eye. The colors were boring. There were no signs. Not everything was priced. It was as if Imogene McAllister Rosenstein just didn't care.

Not even a lick.

Displaying your merchandise, some pointers:

*Cover your tables with attractive fabric, in a solid color which complements your pieces.

In craft show settings, you will find that lighter colors work better than darker ones.

I think it is better to cover the full front of the table with a cloth, not just the top of the table.

*Have pretty containers to hold your wares.

*Think of display in terms of levels. You do not want everything lying flat on a table.

In your booth, you might have a mix of low tables, higher tables, tall heights, stands, pedestals, hanging items.

*Coordinate your use of color with the colors prominent in your business cards, brochures and signage.

A warm, colorful, bright, airy feeling is much better than a dark, cave feeling.

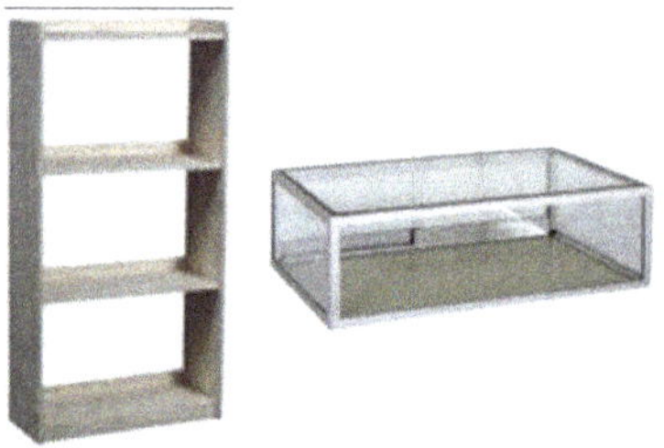

*Open book cases work better than ones with closed backs.

Be careful, if using displays which are glass enclosed, that the glass reflection does not diminish the ability to view jewelry inside these displays.

*Keep things creative, but not complex or cluttered.

Don't let things get barren, either, what I call a "TOOTHLESS LOOK".

Your displays should be attractive, but should not compete for attention with your jewelry. With this in mind, you do not necessarily have to put all your inventory out at once.

Kabana (https://kabana.com/) (https://kabana.com/)

Build displays around these natural focal points.

I loved how this octopus bracelet worked as that key focal point for Kabana Jewelry. Kabana Jewelry had most of their pieces in glass display cases. But they kept this octopus bracelet in a central point on top of their counter.

Boy, did this bracelet ever attract people to their booth. Everyone wanted to touch it and try it on.

CLEANING

Keep your glass clean.

Keep your jewelry shiny.

Keep your booth tidy.

You want that customer at 4pm Sunday to be as excited as that customer was at 1pm the day before.

4. SIGNAGE

First and foremost, follow the show promoter's rules about signage!

Your sign or signs should be visible from all sides of your booth from which customers will be approaching. If the back of your booth will be visible, put a sign there. Put a sign on the inside of your booth. I like to hang a poster-sized image of someone wearing a piece of my jewelry. I imprint my business name on the poster.

Your signs should be simple, clean and with a clear font. The colors red and yellow are seen from the furthest distance away.

Your sign should say what you sell, not necessarily your business name. For example, "JEWELRY TO LOVE" is much better than "IMOGENE'S CREATIONS".

Signs should generate interest and help sell your products.

Don't use "superlatives" like best, most, cheapest, largest and the like.

In as few words as possible, tell the customer how your product will solve his or her problem, or meet his or her needs. Why would your pieces be valuable to someone else? "What you need for that special occasion." "The earrings you always wanted but could never find."

Be positive and diplomatic in your wording. Writing "unruly kids will be sold as slaves" makes the point much better than "No Kids".

Explain that which is not obvious. What's it made of? When using the product, what must be avoided — such as getting it wet? Are there any disclaimers or conditions? What are the advantages of your product over others?

Use colors, typefaces, and images on your sign which have the same feel as your merchandise. Don't overdo your signage, so that the signs overwhelm your inventory.

Be sure you have a clear, prominent sign that includes the name of your business.

If your booths are number, this number should appear on the sign.

Everything in your booth should be tagged, labeled, priced and identified for the customer. Information is important.

You might have **framed little write-ups** sitting with various displays and telling the customer something about yourself, your technique or your jewelry.

Without good and **prominently visible information**, customers often walk away without asking for help.

PRICE TAGS

Everything in your booth should be tagged, labeled, priced and identified for the customer.

Information is important. You might have framed little write-ups sitting with various displays and telling the customer something about yourself, your technique or your jewelry. Without good and prominently visible information, customers often walk away without asking for help.

Price tags are a must. If you have the time and can afford it, use professionally-printed price tags. You can buy label makers now at stationery stores, and with which you can generate printed price tags. Price tags give credence to the price, and reduce the times customers may try to haggle.

TAKE-AWAYS and SIGN-UPS

Have business cards, postcards, brochures, and

newsletters easily available.

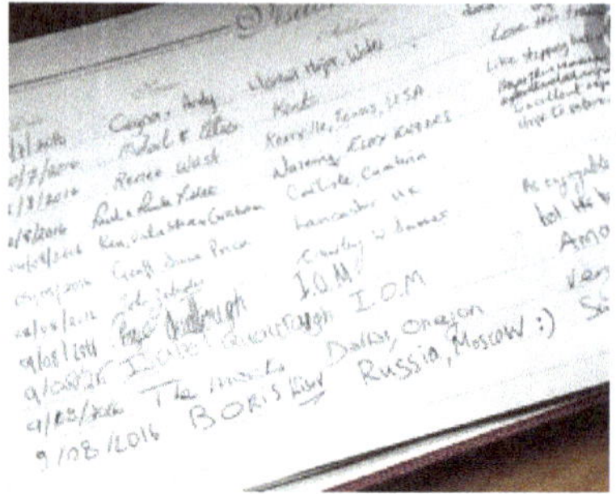

Put out a sign-up book or sign-up sheets to expand your mailing and emailing lists.

5. LOADING AND UN-LOADING

Allow yourself plenty of time to unload and set up your booth. If allowed to drive into the venue to unload, be courteous and unload as quickly as possible. Then move your vehicle before continuing to setup.

I like to modular-ize everything. That is, I like to use similar sized and shaped containers to carry everything in. They are sturdy, easy for one person to carry. The

132

containers are stackable. Each container is clearly labeled on the outside to what is on the inside. Some of my containers to double-time as pedestals or supports for displays. I use other containers for active storage during the show, but easily storable, out of sight of the customers, usually under the table.

If you need a van or truck, and don't own one, these are easily and very inexpensively rentable at local U-Haul or similar business.

LESSON 8:
Bring Enough Inventory To Sell

Remember Rowena Starlight?

She's the one who liked to sell upscale pieces in not-so-upscale settings. She spent so much time making each piece, that she had very little inventory to bring with her. She assumed she would sell out everything she brought, and thus come out ahead. Which is what she never did.

INVENTORY

1. Bring enough inventory to sell, typically 4 times what you hope to sell. Thus, if you want to sell $200.00 (total revenue) of stuff, you would want to bring $800.00 (total retail price) of merchandise.

2. Don't necessarily put everything out at once. You want your booth to look full, abundant and complete, but not cluttered or overwhelming. At the same time you do not want "Empty Spaces" where it looks like you have run out of things to sell. If you started with a large bowl of loose items, and you have sold out half of them, replace that bowl with a smaller bowl.

3. Have merchandise with a variety of price points.

You will want to have a mix of impulse items, as well as more expensive things, and perhaps 2 or 3 very high end art pieces.

4. Think what kinds of jewelry sells the most, and what sells the least. Usually earrings and bracelets sell the most, and necklaces and specialized items sell the least. But this all depends somewhat on current fashions.

5. People carry around with them $1 bills, $5 bills, $10 bills, $20's, $50's and $100's. The impulse buyer is more likely to purchase something in these denominations.

6. Sell things you love.

137

LESSON 9:
Sell Yourself And Your Craft
At The Show

Sarsaparilla Sue was great with customers. She began each conversation by talking about her name. While she was drinking sarsaparilla in a local soda shop, the idea came to her – making jewelry which looked like candy confections. She looked around the shop and noticed all the colors and color combinations. The textures, the visual sensations, and she found materials to match, and designs which expressed all her feelings and creative inspirations.

In that soda shop.
How sweet.
Sweet Sarsaparilla Sue.

SELL YOURSELF *And* YOUR CRAFT

Don't Sit.

If you are allowed, demonstrate your craft

At the show, you are not only selling your products. You are selling *yourself*. Yourself as a jewelry designer. Your creativity. Your personality. The essence of your artistic soul.

You sell yourself to motivate your customers. You want to motivate people to stop by your booth and linger. You want to motivate people to buy. You want to motivate them to remember you and your work. You want them to purchase from you again.

All this motivating will take a lot of work on your part.

1. ***BODY LANGUAGE***

2. ***TELLING YOUR STORY***

3. ***DEMONSTRATING YOUR SKILLS***

4. ***MAKING THE SALE WORK FOR THEM***

The way you sit, the way you stand, your facial expressions, how you greet customers, how you converse with customers, how you describe your work, and your technique. These all subtly affect the shopping experiences and behaviors of your customers.

Part of the selling process is pure theater. You need to put on a good show.

After all, you want to attract customers to your booth. You want them to linger. You want them to ask for help, and ask other questions. You want them to remember you and what you sell.

First, *stand, don't sit.*

If you do need to sit, sit at an angle to your booth or display table, rather than sitting directly centered, facing forward. In this way, people can approach your display without feeling you are watching their every step as they make their way to your booth.

If it's going to be a long day and a long weekend, you might resort to a higher director's chair or stool, as a sort of compromise between standing and sitting to take short breaks.

YOUR FACIAL EXPRESSIONS ARE IMPORTANT

Don't look bored. Don't stare off into space. Don't look like you would rather be somewhere else. Don't stand with your arms folded, or your hands in your pockets. Don't look like your primary mission is to guard your booth.

Look happy. Look eager to meet new people, greet familiar faces, and share your stories and y our work.

141

Be visible, don't hide.

Look busy. When it's slow, do business-related activities:
Clean, Dust, Re-Arrange, Change Out Merchandise, Price, Make Some More Jewelry, Inventory Things, Take Pictures.

ENGAGE PEOPLE AS THEY WALK BY OR APPROACH YOUR BOOTH

Catch their eyes.

Say "GOOD DAY", or "BEAUTIFUL DAY OUT TODAY".

Compliment people, like saying "LOVE THAT NECKLACE," or "BEAUTIFUL SHOES."

Don't Hover

Give your customers some space to shop. Yes, you do have to worry about shop-lifting, but you don't want to make every customer feel like you think they are a crooks.

Don't hover over them. Don't force conversations on them. Don't take away their fun of shopping.

But also, do not ignore them. Greet them. Ask them if they need assistance. Ask them if they would like to try a piece on. Ask them how the show has been going for them.

DRESS THE PART

Be well-groomed. Be presentable. Smell good. But don't bath yourself in cologne. Don't get caught with bad breath. And, in a similar vein, don't eat things which result in bad breath, like onions and tuna fish.

Wear your jewelry.

Wear a name badge.

Don't eat in your booth.

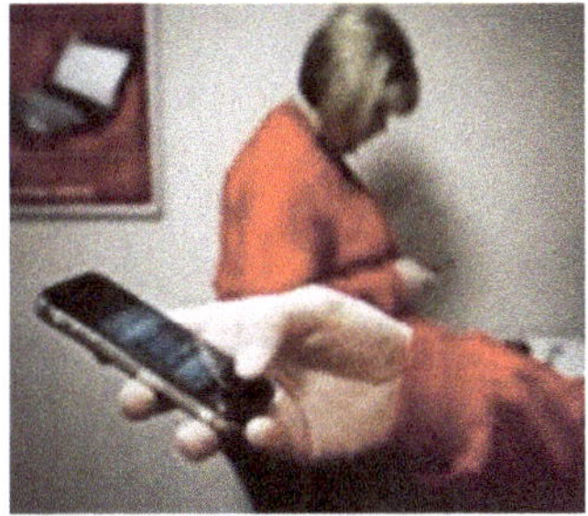

Don't talk on the phone.

Don't text.

Don't smoke.

Don't drink alcoholic beverages.

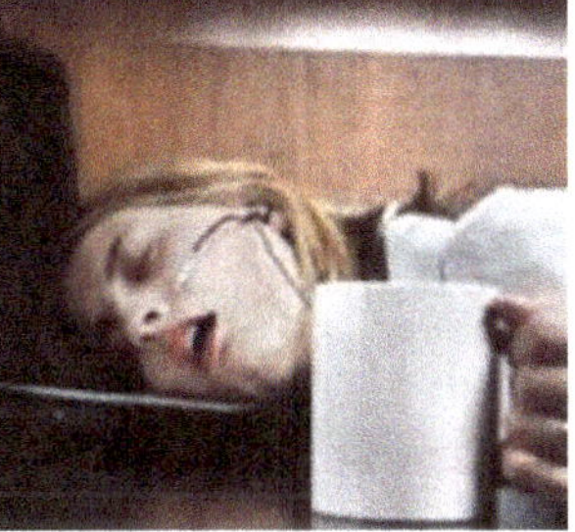

Don't read or sleep.

Don't get lost in conversation with your partner or staff, to the exclusion of your customers.

Don't block the entrance to your booth.

It's a good idea to take breaks about every 4 hours. But don't leave your booth for more than 20 minutes at a time. People want to meet the artist. Your presence is one of your main selling points.

When your booth is crowded, and you have customers

competing for your attention, *acknowledge each one*. Let them know about how long it will before you finish with your existing customer, and can wait on them.

Prioritize.

The person you may be helping might require a lot of time. The next person might require just a few minutes. Excuse yourself from the first person, and wait on the second.

If you have a chatty customer, learn how to politely interrupt, and re-direct the conversation, so that you can smoothly transition to the next customer.

Thank them for the sale

Thank your customers for coming over to your booth.

Be sure they sign a guest register. Be sure they leave with some promotional materials. Be sure they know how to contact you after the show.

If someone has purchased something from you, thank them, then say something like, "*THAT NECKLACE WILL LOOK GREAT ON YOU*," or, "*THAT'S SUCH A THOUGHTFUL GIFT YOU ARE BUYING*," which reinforces the good feelings they have about the purchase, as they hand you the money.

TELL YOUR STORY

Tell your story. When you establish a very personal

connection with your customer, you will more likely make the sale.

People are not just buying your work. They are buying an experience. The more they know about you, your techniques, and the particulars of the work, the more likely they are to buy something.

You, in effect, are building a brand. The brand is you.

Your story should be real, relevant to what you are selling, and repeatable.

Telling her story was something Sarsaparilla Sue did very, very well.

Alford and Selva had a good handle on their business. While they disagreed often on strategy, they negotiated the solutions well. They worked out various stories to tell their customers.

In one of them, Alford told about his career. It went like this:

"Years ago, I drove a truck cross-country. The economy soured, and I was laid off, looking for something else to do. Selva was having some success selling jewelry she made. And I thought we could turn this into a full-fledged business. We began doing flea markets and craft shows, our business took off, and now, even I'm making jewelry. I love it."

SO, YOUR STORY COULD INCLUDE

- IMPORTANT MILESTONES IN YOUR DEVELOPMENT AS AN ARTIST

- HOW YOU GOT STARTED

- HOW YOU LEARNED YOUR "CRAFT"

- WHO TAUGHT YOU

- THE REASONS YOU ARE PASSIONATE ABOUT YOUR WORK

- DO YOU MAKE THINGS FULL TIME OR PART TIME

- YOUR INSPIRATIONS

- INTERESTING FACTS ABOUT THE MATERIALS YOU USE, and WHERE YOU FIND THEM

- SOME HUMOROUS TALES OF THINGS THAT HAPPENED TO YOU, IN THE CONTEXT OF YOUR WORK

- THE KINDS OF THINGS WHICH DIFFERENTIATE YOURSELF FROM OTHER JEWELRY DESIGNERS

- THE KINDS OF THINGS WHICH ARE CRITICAL TO YOUR SUCCESS

- HOW YOU MANAGE A REGULAR JOB AND YOUR "CRAFT"

- WHERE ELSE DO YOU SELL YOUR PIECES

If you are uncomfortable talking about yourself and your jewelry, practice, practice, practice.

WRITE UP YOUR STORY

Make this write-up part of your promotional materials. Tell your story to friends and relatives. Eventually telling your story will become second-nature.

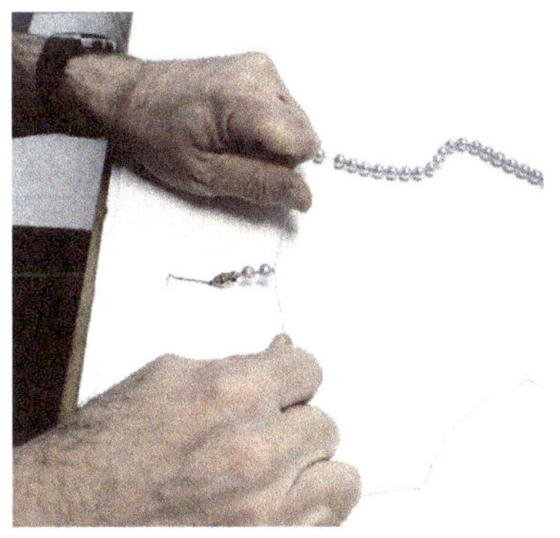

DEMONSTRATE YOUR SKILLS

If the show promoters allow demonstrations, find out their rules.

Demonstrations are great marketing tools. They always attract customers. They get people to linger. They show you really do make your own products.

MAKE THE SALE WORK FOR THEM

Help the customer justify the purchase.

Make it work.

Have tools handy to take out a link or add a link to shorten or lengthen that piece of jewelry.

You may not have exactly what they want. Perhaps you have it in your inventory at home, and you can mail order the sale.

Or, if you do commission work, let people know about this. Explain to them what commission work means, and what your terms are.

CHILDREN CAN DISRUPT THE SALES PROCESS

They can compete for the attention of your customer. They can sometimes wreak havoc with your merchandise and your displays.

I always have some small items to distract them, or something they can fiddle or play with.

Occasionally I spread some beads around on the floor or the ground, and tell children that they can keep what they find. This works well.

LESSON 10:
Make A List Of Things To Bring

Mary and Beth are best friends. Inseparable. Mary is the administrative personality. Beth is the creative one. Beth never understands why Mary makes so many lists, but is always thankful, at the end of each show, that she did.

LISTS

Making lists is one of the only ways I know to keep up with all the details.

Make lists of things to bring for each one of the following:

1. PACKING AND UNPACKING: *storage bins, hand-trucks, bubble wrap*

2. BOOTH SET-UP
    INCLUDING FURNISHINGS AND EQUIPMENT, LIGHTING AND EXTENSION

CORDS

3. INVENTORY

4. MERCHANDISE DISPLAYS
   *INCLUDING, STANDS, RACKS, SHELVING,
   EASELS, TRAYS, TABLECLOTHS, MIRROR*

5. MERCHANDISE PACKAGING SUPPLIES
   SUCH AS BAGS AND TISSUE PAPER

6. MARKETING AND PROMOTION
   *INCLUDING SIGNAGE, BUSINESS CARDS,
   BROCHURES*

7. PERSONAL COMFORT NEEDS
   *SUCH AS DRINKS, FOOD, CHANGES OF
   CLOTHES*

8. FIRST AID
   *INCLUDING BAND-AIDS, ASPIRIN, HAND
   LOTION*

9. CUSTOMER COMFORT NEEDS

10. OFFICE SUPPLIES
    *LIKE PENS, PAPER, STAPLER, TAPE, PRICE
    TAGS, CALCULATORS*

11. MONEY, CREDIT CARD AND SALES
    MANAGEMENT
    *INCLUDING CASH AND CHANGE, FORMS,
    CELL PHONE, CREDIT CARD EQUIPMENT
    CREDIT CARD AUTHORIZATION PHONE
    NUMBERS, SALES TAX CERTIFICATE,*

BUSINESS LICENSE

12. WEATHER AND OTHER CONTINGENCIES
SUPPLIES
*SUCH AS SAFETY PINS, BUNGEE CORDS, ZIP
TIES, SCISSORS, TWINE, TAPE, TENT
WEIGHTS, PLASTIC DROP CLOTHS OR
TARPS, BUG SPRAY, HAT, SUNGLASSES*

13. CLEANING SUPPLIES
*INCLUDING PAPER TOWELS, GLASS
CLEANER, JEWELRY CLEANER, GARBAGE
BAGS*

14. SHOW RELATED
*SUCH AS COPY OF ALL CORRESPONDENCE
WITH SHOW PROMOTER, YOUR
APPLICATION FORM*

15. DEMONSTRATION SUPPLIES
INCLUDING TOOLS

16. SUPPLIES, SAMPLES

17. TOOLS: *Tool Kit For Jewelry Repairs and
Adjustments; All tools needed for setup
requirements (tent, table, displays, signage, and
the like)*

BE SURE TO BRING A CAMERA.

Take pictures of your final booth set-up.

Take pictures of your merchandise displays.

Take pictures of items that seem to be selling well.

LESSON 11:
Be Prepared To Accept Credit Cards

Alford Greene and his wife Selva argued for days on end. He wanted to be able to accept credit cards at craft shows, she thought it was too expensive. Lucky for both of them, the technology today allows for very inexpensive, easy-to-use, credit card systems for you to use at craft shows.

ACCEPTING CREDIT CARDS

You will definitely lose sales, if you do not have a way to accept credit cards.

Today, there are several systems that allow you to put a small attachment onto your cell phone, or portable equipment which will run on Wi-FI if that is available to you. Most of today's art and craft shows make Wi-FI available for a fee. But you may be able to also link up to your cell phone carrier's system without connecting to the local venue's Wi-FI service.

These credit card systems allow you to run credit cards with very small finance charges to you.

It is very quick and easy to get approved.

Equipment needed: You can use your cell phone. You can purchase various scanner devices. You can link up to a portable cash register.

Your cell phone company may have a product for you. Also, there are other types of companies with similar products, called POS or Point Of Sale Systems, like

SQUARE (https://squareup.com/us/en)

GOPAYMENT (https://quickbooks.intuit.com/payments/mobile/)

PAYANYWHERE (https://www.payanywhere.com)

LESSON 12:
Price Things To Sell

You may be interested in my extensive online video tutorial about PRICING AND SELLING YOUR JEWELRY *.
https://so-you-want-to-be-a-jewelry-designer.teachable.com/p/pricing-and-selling-your-jewelry*

In this video tutorial, I share with you my knowledge, experiences and insights about...

1. *Why Jewelry Sells*

2. *Three alternative pricing formulas used by jewelry makers and the jewelry industry*

3. *A simple, mathematical formula for pricing*

your jewelry which I developed and prefer to use, and which gives a range within which to select a price that will be seen as fair and reasonable

4. *How to break down this mathematical pricing formula into a series of easy to implement steps*

5. *How to adjust the formula to compute retail prices or wholesale prices*

Price Things To Sell

Customers who attend different kinds of shows have different kinds of expectations about price. People expect to pay higher prices at Arts and Crafts Shows, and lower prices at Flea Markets and Bazaars.

You always begin by setting fair and reasonable prices.

At higher end shows, you want to minimize any discounting or haggling.

At flea markets, be prepared to haggle.

When you *haggle* on price, in any setting, you would typically be prepared to sell for about 15% less than the marked price.

It's OK to say "NO" to a customer if the customer only

seems willing to pay a very low amount. You would be out of business if you sold all your stuff below what it costs you to make.

If you use my pricing formula (*see video tutorial link above*), the formula will generate a range, showing the minimum and the maximum prices you can charge without under- or over-charging the customer.

LESSON 13:
Keep Your Money Safe

Alford Greene and his wife Selva also argued about how to manage the money at the show. Selva wanted a money box. Alford wanted to keep the money on his person.

In this case, I would side with Alford.

You need to manage your transactions.

Keep your money safe.

Set up an efficient payment station.

Have enough money on hand to make change – 1 and 5 dollar bills, and quarters, dimes, nickels and pennies.

With all the people around competing for your attention, it gets too easy for shop-lifters to steal your money box, or steal your purse, before you notice it's gone.

I like to wear an apron with pockets. I keep enough money in the apron pockets to handle a few hour's worth of sales. I keep the rest of the money in pants pockets or a money belt or fanny pack on my person. You can find handyman's aprons at a local hardware store. These have deep pockets, easily tie off on your body, and work well.

Guy with apron on with pouch for money

****Be especially alert at *set-up* and *break-down* times, when there is a lot of commotion.**

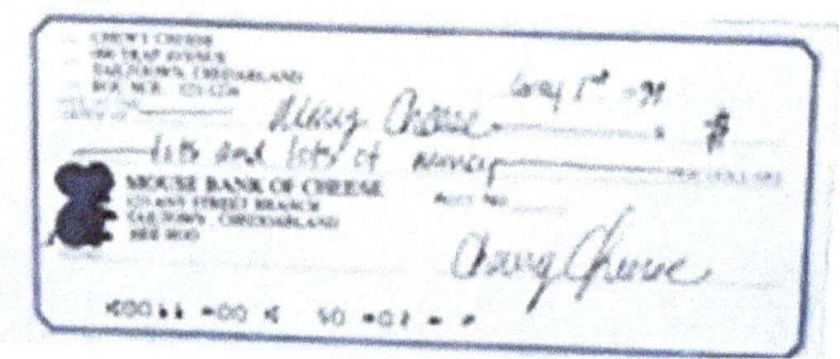

Lots of people pass bad checks. Some people make a career of this. Because of this, I am always leery of accepting checks. Luckily today, many people use their debit cards, in lieu of checks, and these are much safe.

If someone asks if they can write a check, I try to discourage it. I ask them if they can use a debit or credit card, instead.

Occasionally I do accept checks, but rarely these days.

If accepting checks, some yellow flags to watch out for:

- CHECK SEQUENCE NUMBERS BELOW 300
- ANY CHECK FROM ANYONE IN THE MILITARY
- STARTER CHECKS, WHERE THE ADDRESS IS NOT IMPRINTED
- OUT OF STATE CHECKS
- WHERE THE WRITER SHOWS A COLLEGE ID, OR THE ADDRESS IS A COLLEGE DORM

Verify the customer's phone number, and write this on the check.

Also check the customer's driver's license, with picture and signature. And write down the customer's driver's license on the check.

Most banks no longer allow you to verify whether the customer has enough money in their account to cover the check. The few banks that still provide this service, often charge you $5.00 - $25.00 per verification.

CRAFT SHOWS ATTRACT SHOPLIFTERS

There are lots of people, lots of commotion, and lots of distractions.

You find yourself in a new, unfamiliar environment. These kinds of things make shoplifting easier to get away with. Shoplifters come in all sizes, shapes, ages, genders and colors. They may try to stuff some jewelry into a large purse or bag or coat pocket, and walk away without paying. They may try a piece of jewelry on, and walk away without paying. They may grab and run.

Often, they work in pairs, one person to distract you,

and the other person to steal you blind while you are not looking.

Tell-Tale Characteristics of shoplifters:

- SEEM NERVOUS, REFUSE OFFERS OF ASSISTANCE

- SPEND AN INORDINATE AMOUNT OF TIME WATCHING SALES STAFF, RATHER THAN LOOKING AT MERCHNDISE

- MAKE AN ESPECIALLY HURRIED EXIT

- WEAR OVERCOATS, BAGGY CLOTHES, CARRY OVERSIZED PURSES

- GROUPS OF TEENAGERS OR TWEEN-AGERS SHOPPING TOGETHER

- LOITER

Shoplifters require some level of privacy in order to conceal merchandise. So, in anticipation of this, you will want to:

- Maximize visibility from all places in your area

- Minimize blind spots from all places in your area

- From where you are standing or sitting, you should have good sight lines throughout the areas in your booth your customer has access to

- Lock up shoplifter attractive merchandise, or keep it behind the counter

As a general rule, the smaller and more valuable an item, the more attractive target it is.

What proportion of merchandise should you keep

under glass? There is no rule of thumb here. You have to use your judgment.

Keep everything in its place. This makes it easier to monitor things, because, if everything has its place, and you keep putting things back in the same place, you are more likely to notice, and notice more quickly, if things are out of order.

If you put items in a bag, staple it closed. Staple the receipt to the bag. You can even staple one of your business cards to the bag.

Require a receipt for all returns.

One thing some shoplifters like to do is steal something, and then return it for cash.

The most effective thing you can do to prevent shoplifting is to provide exceptional customer service.

- Acknowledge each customer

- Ask if they need assistance.

If you suspect or catch a shoplifter, immediately notify the show's security. You want to describe the suspect, whether you think he or she is still present, whether they

173

might be causing trouble, and what the suspect looks like and is wearing.

FINE JEWELRY

Jewelers selling fine jewelry, particularly with gold and precious stones, need to take special precautions.

Don't work alone. You should have one or more people with you in the booth at all times.

If you feel that anyone is casing you, alert the show authorities.

You might take a picture of anyone suspicious with your cell phone or disposable camera.

Don't register at the hotel using your business name.

Don't take a first floor room.

Don't take a room near an elevator or stairs.

When you checkout of the hotel, you want to drive a long distance before stopping for food or gas. Be sure you have a full gas-tank before that last day at the show.

Keep your money on your person.

If you have valuable merchandise or money in containers, keep these chained to something immovable, like a support column in the room.

ABOUT HIRING HELP

Be careful about hiring non-show people who happen to be around the show at set-up, and offer to help for money.

If you need to hire extra help, try to arrange this ahead of time.

Does the show promoter keep of list of local people to contact? Can you contact local craft, bead or jewelry stores to ask for recommendations? How about a local craft association or bead society? How about other vendors – do they know someone locally that they used before? You can also contact some local temporary services.

OTHER SECURITY CONCERNS:

Don't leave tempting items in your booth overnight.

Lock your vehicle. Be sure all the doors are locked – front, back, sides.

Be sure all your windows are closed.

RECORD KEEPING

176

Date	Origin - Destination	Odometer	Total Miles	Purpose of Travel

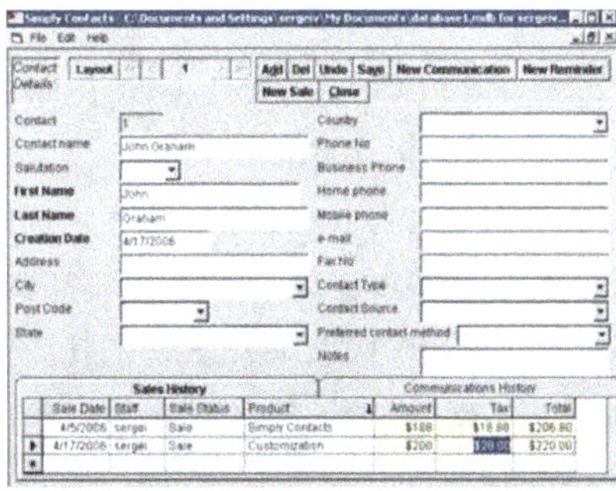

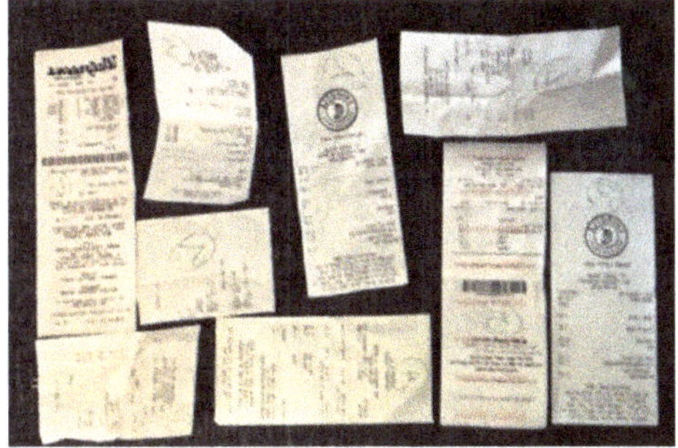

RECORD KEEPING IS VERY IMPORTANT

Keep good records of your sales. Differentiate by type of sale: retail, wholesale, discounted, consignment.

Keep good records of customer mail, email addresses.

Keep good records and receipts of expenses incurred

and other associated costs.

Keep good records of car mileage associated with your show related travel.

If you will be collecting sales taxes, be sure you are collecting all the information you need to fill out any government sale tax forms.

If you are selling wholesale, be sure your customers are presenting you with the correct tax id numbers and documents. Write their tax ID number down on their receipt. The state you are doing business in will probably have a form for them to fill out, and which you save. There is also a universal sales tax form you can download and use.

If you are in a state that collects sales taxes, you will need to collect sales taxes at the show.

You may have a permanent re-sale number in that state. Some states call these tax numbers or wholesale numbers.

If so, you would pay the sales taxes you have collected to the state as you always do.

If you have a temporary state re-sale license that covers the time at the show, you will be given a form by the state with which to transmit payment for collected taxes.

Sometimes, state officials will be at the show, going booth to booth, to collect your sales taxes. If so, they expect you to have completed your form, meaning you have calculated all your taxable and non-taxable sales, as well as the total sales taxes owed, as you are closing down your booth, and beginning to pack up.

Other times, you are expected to submit that form with payment usually within 2-4 weeks of the show.

Nowadays, a lot of this process is done online.

Be sure you have the instructions about what you need to do when.

LESSON 14:
Generate Follow-Up Sales

YOU MAKE YOUR REAL MONEY THROUGH REPEAT BUSINESS

Much of this repeat business occurs between shows.

Some of it occurs when people, who bought from you at one show, return to your booth at the next one.

Or buys from you online.

Or visits your shop.

Some of it occurs as the result of word-of-mouth, where your customer lets other people know about you and they then buy from you.

Notify your existing customers where you will be when. Either emailing them or mailing out postcards works fine.

For regular or very good customers, you might try phoning them.

Also, you should have some kind of web presence and/or physical store presence where the customer can easily find you between shows.

Guest Book

DURING THE SHOW...

- Have a guest register or sign-up sheet, to generate mail and email address

- Have at least 2-3 takeaway promotional items, such as business cards, brochures, postcards

Be sure, on each of your promotional handouts, you clearly list how the customer can get in touch with you between shows.

Also, I like to have some kind of give-away, where people fill out a form with their address information, say to win a free piece of jewelry.

Some people like to give away promotional items with their business names imprinted on them.

- Update your mailing and emailing databases

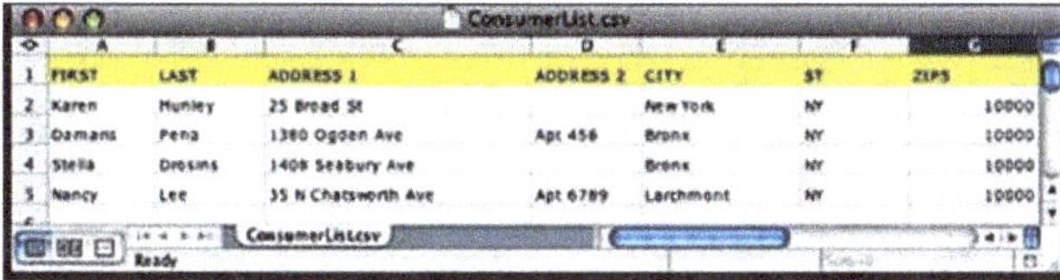

- Follow up at least with those customers who made a purchase, using email or mail and thanking them

- Do some evaluation. Write down what things to keep or keep doing, and what things did not sell that well.

Ask yourself: Why or Why Not? If you can structure in any customer or other vendor feedback, that would be very helpful.

- Return to your breakeven analysis. How much money did you actually make? Was it worthwhile? If you spent $1,000, did you make at least $1,000 back?

LESSON 15:
Take Care Of Yourself

Take care of yourself at the show. Shows are exciting, but also can be physically and emotionally exhausting.

If it's possible to bring someone along to help you, do so.

Be sure you work out the details for food breaks and bathroom breaks.

Bring food to snack on, water to drink, any medications you need, at the least, some aspirin.

Anticipate the weather, and whether it will change during the day, or over the days of the show. Bring clothes, hats, sunglasses, sweaters, sun-block, bug-spray – whatever.

Always think in terms of layers of clothing. You may want different clothes to wear when setting up, than when staffing your booth. You may want a change of clothes, particularly if the days are hot and humid.

I can't emphasize enough: **Wear Comfortable Shoes!**

LESSON 16:
Be Nice To Your Neighbors

Make friends with your neighbors. Your neighbors may become some of your best business resources.

Ask about their products. Ask about their experiences with craft shows. Send customers their way. Exchange business hints and craft show opportunities.

Offer to watch their booths when they need to take a break.

Listen to how they manage sales and customers.

As you walk around the show, pay attention to good booth and display ideas.

Open your booth on time.

Santa's Bag Arts & Crafts Show
A fundraiser for The Fountain Clinic
Marshall High School
701 N. Marshall Avenue
Marshall, MI 49068

RULES and GUIDELINES

1. Hours are 9:00 AM to 4:00 PM.
   a. Set up begins at 6:00 AM. You may not set up the night before and we cannot grant any requests for an earlier set up.

2. All items are to be handcrafted by the seller
   a. Objectionable material, or material not as represented, will be removed.
   b. No commercial products are allowed; if they are mixed in with home-crafted products the vendor will be asked to leave and will not be asked to return to future shows.
   c. Plastic canvas, ceramics & items made from kits are not acceptable.

3. Cancellations made up to a month before the show will get a full refund. Any cancellation made within 30 days of the show will receive a refund.
   a. There will be NO refunds for "no shows" and such vendors will not be asked to return to future shows.

4. Booth Guidelines:
   a. Tables should be skirted or covered with tablecloths.
   b. If you indicated you need electricity (which is not guaranteed) you are responsible for bringing your own extension cords.
   c. You are responsible for the sales tax at your booth.

If you have any questions regarding the guidelines of this craft show, please contact Cheryl Hinds at:
(269) 789.0410 or chinds@fountain-clinic.org

Please keep this list along with your acceptance letter as your reference for the show.

Don't start packing up and closing your booth until the show officially closes.

Be sensitive to the needs of the handicapped.

Stick within the "lines" of your space.

Be sure you have conformed to local, state and federal rules.

Respect limits on smoking, drinking, eating and playing music.

Booth Etiquette / Following Event Guidelines

If you sign a contract to do a show, you are agreeing to follow all the guidelines and stipulations. Don't whine or complain. The show owners have a lot to deal with. You don't want to get yourself banned from future shows.

Stay within your space. If you need a slightly large space, either *buy it* ahead of time from the show promoters, or negotiate an arrangement with your neighbor. You don't want to make enemies with your neighbors. You don't want to make it difficult and uncomfortable for your customers to view your merchandise. You don't want to alienate the show's promoters.

Don't pack up early. Wait until the very end of the show.

Be aware of any restrictions about smoking and eating in your booth, or in the general exhibit area.

Some Final Words of Advice

SOME FINAL WORDS OF ADVICE

Doing craft shows is a wonderful experience. You can make a lot of money at craft shows, you meet new people, you have new adventures. You learn a lot about business and arts and crafts designing.

IF... you do your homework when selecting them, and verify all information, and,

IF... you are very organized in preparing for them, setting up, selling and re-packing up, and,

IF... you promote, promote, promote.

One of the first things I tell anyone who wants to get into this business is to give it 3 years. If you are still struggling after 3 years, perhaps craft shows are not for you.

Each year, you will do some shows, and some will work, and others might not.

Avoid first time events. I usually avoid shows in existence less than 3 years.

Try to do events others have told you have been successful for them.

I give many shows a second chance, *if* I feel the major issues for slow sales were timing or weather.

Don't feel disappointed if you didn't make a fortune your first time out. Remember, it's that repeat business where you make the most money.

KEEP ME POSTED ABOUT YOUR SUCCESS

I wanted to share with you lessons I have learned over the years about doing craft shows.

I am confident, that with a little homework and organization, you can make craft shows a successful venue for selling your work.

If you have any questions, or if you want to share any of your experiences, you can always reach me through my website – warrenfeldjewelry.com.

Thank you again.

Best of luck with your craft show business.

For *SO YOU WANT TO BE A JEWELRY DESIGNER...* ,

I'm **WARREN FELD**

warren@warrenfeldjewelry.com

Helpful Resources

HELPFUL RESOURCES:

CHECK OUT THESE RESOURCES AND THEIR WEB-LINKS

ONLINE DIRECTORIES:

FESTIVAL NETWORK ONLINE
http://festivalnet.com/
Searchable database listing 24,000+ north American events; show ratings. Database includes fine arts fairs, arts and craft shows, music festivals, expos, corporate events, and more.

SHOWLISTER

http://www.showlister.com/

Searchable database of event listings. Art and craft shows, street fairs, festivals, home and garden shows, holiday gift shows, special events, farmers' markets, state & county fairs, trade shows and more.

NATIONAL CRAFT SHOWS DIRECTORY

http://www.nationalcraft shows.com/

Craft show listings by state

CRAFTS FAIR ONLINE

http://www.craftsfaironline.com/

Listings of shows. The Crafts Fair online is the oldest and largest directory of crafts oriented sites on the web. We offer organized links to thousands of individual crafter's web sites as well as craft web malls, crafts organizations, supplies, listings of real world shows, craft publications, instruction, software and more. In The Crafter's Web Development Center we offer all the information and resources crafts people need to create their own independent web sites.

ART FESTIVAL

http://www.artfestival.com/

Listing of Howard Alan Events & American Craft Endeavors around the US. Art fair promoter.

SOUTHERN FESTIVALS

http://www.southfest.com/

Listing of festivals in southern US. Lists festivals and events in the South including Georgia, Texas, North Carolina,

South Carolina, Florida, Louisiana, Tennessee and Virginia.

SUNSHINE ARTIST

http://www.sunshineartist.com/

Listing of shows in US with reviews. Since 1972, *Sunshine Artist* has provided its readers with comprehensive reviews of everything from fine art fairs, festivals and events, to small craft shows around the country, focusing on all aspects of the shows from sales to artist amenities to the quality of art or craft. We also include in each issue hundreds of art and craft show listings, including contacts, booth fees, application deadlines and the type of art/craft that the event accepts. Finally, in each issue you'll find features on everything from tips to boost your business to in-depth reports on current trends on the show circuit.

ART FAIR CALENDAR

http://www.artfaircalendar.com/

Listings of US and Canada shows. Art fair event listings nationwide, **including** fine art shows **virtually online.**

CRAFTMASTER NEWS

http://www.craftmasternews.com/

Listings of shows in US. Art and craft shows, street fairs, festivals, home and garden shows, holiday gift shows, special events, farmers' markets, state & county fairs, trade shows and more.

PROFESSIONAL CRAFTERS

(www.professionalcrafters.com)

Craft industry news, hot trends, marketing strategies and creative techniques .Cutting edge resources and inside information to take your craft business to the next level and beyond. Join worldwide network of Art and Craft industry professionals and access the news and views.

FAIRS AND FESTIVALS.net

Find Art Shows, Craft Shows, and Festivals near you (fairsandfestivals.net) (https://www.fairsandfestivals.net/) "We believe strongly in the creativity and capability of the independent business person and are excited to be a part of the new American Renaissance being built by artisans, crafters, concessionaires and entrepreneurs." Up-to-date detailed event information for your show calendars. Multiple sales and marketing channels for increased exposure. Expert tools, and educational resources for learning more about the industry. Trusted partners to helping you network with peers and contacts that can help you build your business.

ART AND CRAFT SHOW YELLOW PAGES

Craft Shows, Art & Craft Fairs, Street Fairs and Festivals in All States (artscraftsshowbusiness.com)
Helping artists, crafters and vendors find events in the Eastern US where they can sell their works or products.

ART FAIR SOURCE BOOK

Art Fair and Craft Show Listings | Art Fair SourceBook (https://artfairsourcebook.com/)
AFSB is an online tracking system that organizes 285,420

facts into an easy- to-use, powerful planning tool. With AFSB's critiques you'll be able to target the best shows for your style of work and price range.

ETSY TEAMS

https://www.etsy.com/teams
The Teams section of the ETSY site
(https://www.etsy.com/teams) has groups located throughout the U.S. and each team has its own forum where members interact. Many local teams have an ongoing thread that lists upcoming events of interest to crafters.

EVENTBRITE

Eventbrite - Discover Great Events or Create Your Own & Sell Tickets (https://www.eventbrite.com/)

CHECK OUT **FACEBOOK COMMUNITY PAGES**

ONLINE APPLICATION SERVICES:

JURIED ART SERVICES

juriedartservices.com/
A digital juried and application system. Jurors can view the artists' work along with accompanying descriptions and

dimensions. Because they are self-paced, jurors have the time they need to properly review each application. The artist controls the layout of the works and sees exactly what the jurors see. The process is the most efficient and proven method available for the artists, shows and jurors.

ZAPPLICATION

https://www.zapplication.org/

A digital juried and application system. ZAPP enables artists to apply online to multiple art shows through one central website, ZAPPlication.org. The online application process also allows artists to directly upload digital images of their artwork for jury review. The result is that all artwork in the system is in a consistent, high-quality, digital format. The digital images are presented to the jurors of each show and the system allows them to score online.

ALSO, CHECK WITH YOUR
LOCAL AND STATEWIDE ARTS COMMISSIONS

AND,
STATEWIDE OR LOCAL CRAFT ASSOCIATIONS

AND,
STATEWIDE OR LOCAL PARKS COMMISSIONS

Thank You
and,
Request For Reviews

A Note from Warren Feld

Thank you so much for reading *So You Want To Do Craft Shows.*

If you enjoyed it, please take a moment to leave a review at your favorite online retailer such as Amazon USA or Amazon UK, or social media site.

I welcome contact from readers. At my website, you can contact me, sign up for my intermittent emails, purchase my jewelry and my kits, read my articles and blog and find me on social networking.

http://www.warrenfeldjewelry.com

-- Warren Feld

About Warren Feld, Jewelry Designer

*For **Warren Feld**, Jewelry Designer, (www.warrenfeldjewelry.com), beading and jewelry making have been wonderful adventures. These adventures have taken Warren from the basics of bead stringing and bead weaving, to pearl knotting, micro-macrame, wire working, wire weaving and silversmithing, and onward to more complex jewelry designs which build on the strengths of a full range of technical skills and experiences.*

What excites Warren is finding answers to such questions as:

- What does it mean to be fluent and literate in design?

- What are the implications for defining jewelry as an "object" versus as an "intent"?

- Why does some jewelry draw your attention, and others do not?

- How does jewelry design differ from art or craft?

- How do you judge a piece as finished and successful?

In 2000, Warren founded The Center for Beadwork & Jewelry Arts (CBJA) as the educational program for Be Dazzled Beads-Land of Odds in Nashville, Tennessee. The program approaches education from a Design Perspective. There is a strong focus on skills development. There is a major emphasis on teaching how to make better choices when selecting beads, other parts and stringing materials, and how to bring these altogether into a beautiful, yet functional, piece of jewelry. There are requirements for sequencing classes – that is, taking classes in a developmental order. Jewelry Design is seen as an authentic performance task. As such, the student explores ideas about artistic intent, shared understandings among all audiences, and developing evidence in design sufficient for determining whether a piece is finished and successful.

Warren leads a group of instructors at Be Dazzled Beads (www.bedazzledbeads.com). He teaches many of the bead-weaving, bead-stringing, pearl and hand knotting, wire weaving, jewelry design and business-oriented courses. He works with people just getting started with beading and jewelry making, as well as those with more experience.

His pieces have appeared in beading and jewelry magazines and books, including Perlen Posie ("Gwynian Ropes Bracelet", No. 21, 2014), Showcase 500 Beaded Jewelry ("Little Tapestries: Ghindia", Lark Publications, 2012). One piece ("Canyon Sunrise"), which won 4th place in Swarovski's *Naturally Inspired Competition* (2008), is in the SwarovskI museum in Innsbruck, Austria. His work has been written up in *The Beader's Guide to Jewelry Design* (Margie Deeb, Lark Publications, 2014). He has been a faculty member at CraftArtEdu.com, developing video tutorials.

He was selected as an instructor for the Bead & Button Show, June, 2019, teaching 3 pieces – Japanese Garden Bracelet, Etruscan Square Stitch Bracelet, and ColorBlock Bracelet. In March 2020, Warren led a travel-enrichment program on Celebrity Cruise Lines, centered on jewelry making, beginning with a cruise from Miami to Cozumel and Key West.

Personal style: multi-method, intricate color play, adaptive of traditions to contemporary design, experimental.

Warren is currently working on these books: SO YOU WANT TO BE A JEWELRY DESIGNER, and CONQUERING THE CREATIVE MARKETPLACE and PEARL KNOTTING...WARREN'S WAY.

Owner, Be Dazzled Beads in Nashville, and Land of Odds (https://www.landofodds.com) (https://www.landofodds.com).

He is probably best known for creating the international The Ugly Necklace Contest, where good jewelry designers attempt to overcome our pre-wired brains' fear response for resisting anything Ugly. He has also sponsored All Dolled Up: Beaded Art Doll Competition and The Illustrative Beader: Beaded Tapestry Competition.

Articles on Medium.com (https://warren-29626.medium.com/)

Jewelry Making Kits For Sale (http://www.warrenfeldjewelry.com/wfjkits.htm)

Artist Statement (http://www.warrenfeldjewelry.com/wfjartiststatement.html)

Teaching Statement (http://www.warrenfeldjewelry.com/pdf/TEACHING%20STATEMENT.pdf)

Portfolio
(http://www.warrenfeldjewelry.com/pdf/PORTFOLIO.pdf)

Testimonials
(http://www.warrenfeldjewelry.com/pdf/TESTIMONIALS.pdf)

Video Tutorials
(https://so-you-want-to-be-a-jewelry-designer.teachable.com/)

Design Philosophy
(http://www.warrenfeldjewelry.com/wfjdesignapproach.htm)

warren@warrenfeldjewelry.com
www.warrenfeldjewelry.com

Other Articles and Tutorials

Thank you. I hope you found this book helpful.

Also, check out my website (www.warrenfeldjewelry.com).

Enroll in my jewelry design and business of craft Video Tutorials online. (https://so-you-want-to-be-a-jewelry-designer.teachable.com)
 Orientation To Beads & Jewelry Findings
 Basics of Bead Stringing and Attaching Clasps
 Pearl Knotting... Warren's Way
 The Jewelry Designer's Approach To Color
 So You Want To Do Craft Shows...
 Naming Your Business
 Pricing And Selling Your Jewelry

Articles on Medium.com
(https://warren-29626.medium.com/)

Articles on Art Jewelry Forum
(https://artjewelryforum.org/library/author/warren-feld/)

Other Books by Warren Feld:

So You Want To Be A Jewelry Designer
https://www.amazon.com/So-You-Want-Jewelry-Designer/dp/B09Y3VNNMW/ref=sr_1_1?crid=1PX5B1WJJM0U5&keywords=warren+feld+so+you+want+to+be+a+jewelry+designer&qid=1655572853&sprefix=warren+feld+so+you+want+to+b%2Caps%2C241&sr=8-1

Conquering The Creative Marketplace
https://www.amazon.com/Conquering-Creative-Marketplace-Fickleness-Business/dp/B0BS8RZXGM/ref=sr_1_1?crid=1VZ1SSRWDWKA3&keywords=warren+feld+conquering&qid=1697651057&sprefix=warren+feld+conquering%2Caps%2C83&sr=8-1&ufe=app_do%3Aamzn1.fos.d977788f-1483-4f76-90a3-786e4cdc8f10

Pearl Knotting...Warren's Way
https://www.amazon.com/dp/B09SBNJTFN

Basics of Bead Stringing and Attaching Clasps
https://www.amazon.com/Basics-Bead-Stringing-Attaching-Clasps/dp/B0BZFNTZTR/ref=sr_1_1?crid=EHN3H7CKL4

00&keywords=warren+feld+basics+of+bead&qid=1697651
122&sprefix=warren+feld+basics+of+bead%2Caps%2C72&
sr=8-1&ufe=app_do%3Aamzn1.fos.d977788f-1483-4f76-
90a3-786e4cdc8f10